To Form A More Perfect Union

Campus Diversity Initiatives

Caryn McTighe Musil, Mildred García, Cynthia A. Hudgins,
Michael T. Nettles, William E. Sedlacek, and Daryl G. Smith

AAC&U is grateful to the following organizations for their financial support, which made this publication possible: the Ford Foundation, the William and Flora Hewlett Foundation, the James Irvine Foundation, the W.K. Kellogg Foundation, the Lilly Endowment, and the Philip Morris Companies Inc.

ASSOCIATION OF AMERICAN COLLEGES AND UNIVERSITIES

Washington, D.C.

Published by
Association of American Colleges and Universities
1818 R Street, NW
Washington, DC 20009, telephone 202/387-3760
www.aacu-edu.org

ISBN 0-911696-78-4

This monograph is the first in a series of three publications that are part of AAC&U's project,
"Understanding the Difference Diversity Makes: Assessing Campus Diversity Initiatives."

Contents

Members of the Diversity Evaluators Collaborative

Mildred García, Associate Vice Provost and Associate Professor of Social and Behavioral Sciences, Arizona State University West

Cynthia A. Hudgins, Senior Research Associate, School of Social Work, University of Michigan

Caryn McTighe Musil, Project Director and Vice President, Education and Diversity Initiatives, Association of American Colleges and Universities

Michael T. Nettles, Professor of Education, University of Michigan, and Executive Director, Frederick D. Patterson Research Institute of the College Fund/UNCF

William E. Sedlacek, Professor of Education and Assistant Director, Counseling Center, University of Maryland

Daryl G. Smith, Professor of Education and Psychology, Claremont Graduate University

AAC&U Support Staff

Brinton S. Ramsey, Project Manager and Program Associate, Education and Diversity Initiatives, AAC&U, 1998-1999

Lee Harper, Project Manager and Program Associate, Education and Diversity Initiatives, AAC&U, 1996-1998

"Worlds I Would Have Never Known"

student, Luther College

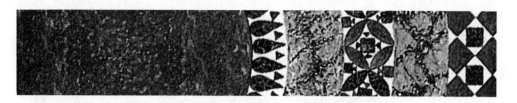

Preface to the Series

They came for religious freedom, and they came to make their fortunes. They came willingly, and they came in chains. They came as aristocrats, as adventurers, and as indentured servants. And when they arrived, the "new world" was already populated by a widely diverse indigenous population. Diversity has always been a part of this nation, even before the United States was defined as a nation. We proudly claimed it as our strength and etched our past and future national character with the phrase whose vision of unity challenges us today: *e pluribus unum*, out of many, one.

While higher education has long been one of the contested sites of experimentation with diversity, the past three decades have been witness to an historically defining moment. Campuses have been the cauldron where newly expanded access has converged with intellectual ferment. In the heat of transmuting its central educational mission, the academy has brimmed with the challenge of making democratic promises become actual practice. Policy innovations, scholarly investigations, and practical experiments have coalesced into what is becoming known as the "campus diversity movement." This movement has focused new attention on access, recruitment, admission, and retention; diversifying faculty, staff, and administrations; restructuring the curriculum; re-evaluating counseling, career planning, and residential life; and re-configuring the relationship between the campus and the community.

Both federal and state governments, philanthropic foundations, private corporations, and academic institutions themselves have provided funding to support these initiatives. The campus diversity movement is the result, above all, of the deep commitment of practitioners who believe diversity is an educational, national, and global resource. Since 1990, however, five foundations and a corporate giving program have assumed national and regional leadership in these efforts. All six have included curricular and campus climate diversity initiatives among their funding priorities and have been an important source of external financial support to academic institutions seeking to make diversity more integral to their educational mission. Between them, these foundations and companies have invested millions of dollars in colleges and universities to promote academic excellence through creating more inclusive educational communities. The six programs that have directly or indirectly assisted more than 500 colleges and universities include:

> the Ford Foundation's Campus Diversity Initiative
> the William and Flora Hewlett Foundation's Pluralism and Unity Program
> the James Irvine Foundation's Higher Education Diversity Initiative
> the W. K. Kellogg Foundation's Centers of Excellence Program
> the Lilly Endowment Inc.'s Improving Racial and Ethnic Diversity and Campus
> Climate at Four-Year Independent Midwest Colleges Program
> the Philip Morris Companies Inc.'s Tolerance on Campus: Establishing Common
> Ground Program.

This monograph, the first in a series of three, is the result of a collaboration of six scholars and evaluators who served as consultants to five of these initiatives. The collaboration began at a meeting convened in February 1995 in Ann Arbor, Michigan, with the support of four foundation program officers. At our first meeting we shared our respective preliminary evaluation reports of campus diversity initiatives prepared for the separate funding agencies. Soon, we moved far beyond simply sharing findings. We pooled our specific campus-based insights to pose more overarching questions about diversity projects in general. Our meetings evolved from discrete reports about diversity activities on specific campuses to a broader discussion of questions implicit in assessing diversity initiatives anywhere. In the process, we became convinced that the campus diversity field would benefit from a collective picture of what was occurring on college campuses. We also believed that we could provide tools that would persuade more people to collect data documenting the strengths and weaknesses of diversity initiatives in order to enhance the quality of higher education.

As we discussed our findings, we were repeatedly reminded of the many differences that we brought to our work. Our interaction was a microcosm of diversity dynamics on college campuses. We were from different parts of the country. We were current or former administrators, faculty members, researchers, and one graduate student. We came from academic affairs, student affairs, and other central administrative offices. We were trained in different disciplines. Some of us had a community college background, and others four-year college and university backgrounds. We were African American, Latina, and European American. We were men and women. What kept us in committed conversation was our collective determination to gain as full a picture as possible of the emerging patterns, insights, and lessons from the extraordinary experimentation taking place on campuses across the United States regarding diversity. We needed the perspectives of all of us in order to do that.

The differences we brought to our work informed our views of diversity, of evaluation, and of the important relationship between the two. We had passionate discussions about what constitutes data, and we debated about issues of confidentiality. Some members of the evaluation team winced at expressions such as "voice," while others flinched at the phrase "percent of variance explained." But all of us understood, throughout the discussions, the richness of multiple, simultaneous vantage points on a single subject of inquiry. Eventually, we also were unanimous that it was not a question of selecting *either* quantitative *or* qualitative methods but how to use *both* in order to enrich the whole. We hungered for more stories to capture the campus drama and for more numbers to analyze progress. Rather than being an impediment, our differences became an asset to our work.

As we wrote our monograph, we quickly confronted the question of language, struggling with the way words themselves are laden with history, context, and vantage point. We recognized their inadequacy, their contested nature, their varying meanings over time and within different communities. Do we use the word "minority" or "people of color"? When we use the word "women," does it only convey "white women"? Does the word "American" suggest an appropriation by the United States that erases the other Americas to our north and south? We have settled on an uneasy compromise in our choices. Our discussions embodied the challenge of taking difference seriously and of learning how to move along in our common task, even if everything is not, or cannot be, fully resolved.

We decided, therefore, to work together more formally in a collaborative project we called "Understanding the Difference Diversity Makes: Assessing Campus Diversity Initiatives." The project itself is the result of an unusual collaboration of the six funding agencies. The centerpiece of the project is a series of three monographs. The monographs are a product of many hearts, hands, and spirits, especially those of students, faculty, staff, and administrators at hundreds of campuses across the country that we visited or whose words we read in reports. Seeking verification and critique directly from the field, we structured a series of six roundtable discussions during the course of the project, three with diversity practitioners who were faculty and administrators and three with campus presidents. Drafts of all three monographs were widely shared and the feedback influential in our final version. The series is also the product of our collective insights as diversity evaluators, our separate research and publications, and the lessons we have gathered from the field over several decades. We believe there is a pressing educational need to reflect more systematically, thoughtfully, and creatively about the progress made thus far in making our campuses more equitable and inclusive. We hope our work will foster that by developing principles, indicators, and instruments to assist the faculty members and administrators we call "campus diversity practitioners."

This first monograph in the series, *To Form a More Perfect Union: Campus Diversity Initiatives*, draws upon research findings that chart the efforts of colleges and universities to move from the rhetoric of inclusion to the practice of equity. We will argue that the current flurry of activity is part of a much longer democratic tradition in higher education, one that has gradually and often only under pressure made a college education available to more people on an equal basis. Such progress, we suggest, moves us from democratic aspiration towards democratic practice. Fueling this movement is a multifaceted rationale, explored in the second chapter, that has caused the majority of institutions to integrate the value of diversity into their mission statements. In response to the swirl of historical and social forces shaping the last four decades, the rationale to diversify has moved far beyond simply eliminating clear race or sex discrimination. It now embraces a complex understanding of how diversity is integral to educational excellence. Increasingly, campuses understand that they must graduate students prepared to thrive in a multicultural and interdependent world. The viability of a robust and strong democracy depends on it, and the demands of a global economy require it.

At the heart of this volume, the third chapter seeks to capture the dazzling array of diversity initiatives put in place on campuses all over the country. They have not always been successful, central, or uncontested. There is no denying, however, that attention to diversity has marked this period in higher education's history. At this juncture, there is new sophistication, deeper levels of understanding, concrete programs tested over time, and a wealth of institutional knowledge about what works, what doesn't, and why. Drawing on interviews, campus visits, and in-depth reports, this chapter etches a portrait of the new academy as it finds itself reinvigorated and challenged by its far more democratic student profile as well as the far more varied intellectual streams on which our understandings of the world are based. Through individual institutional examples a collective pattern of national trends becomes apparent, especially in those areas where the most investment in diversity has occurred.

The basis of our research has come from the campuses engaged directly in diversity work. We have therefore woven specific examples from various colleges and universities throughout the monograph. Under the terms of the Lilly Endowment evaluation report, for reasons of confidentiality, no actual institutional names were used. The names of Lilly-funded schools disguise the name even though these illustrations are drawn from an actual campus. The other evaluation reports to funding agencies, however, had no such restrictions. As a result, most of the references to schools actually identify a particular institution.

In the final chapter, the focus shifts to underscoring the value and significance of assessing diversity work in spite of the difficulty or the unfamiliarity some may have with the task. We argue that the insights are necessary to maintain the quality of the programs, and the evidence is important for the general public to know, particularly in light of the assault on diversity and multiculturalism over the past decade. *Assessing Campus Diversity Initiatives*, the monograph described below, was written to make that enterprise easier. This first monograph is written to assist diversity practitioners, institutional leaders, foundation and corporate funders, and concerned members of the public to understand the emerging mosaic of campus diversity initiatives.

The second volume, *Assessing Campus Diversity Initiatives*, is the book that people in the field have been eager for. It is a practical guide to assessing diversity projects. Because diversity both depends on traditional methods of evaluation and requires inventing methods more appropriate to the subject matter, the handbook offers guiding principles particularly relevant to diversity. It is organized to provide step-by-step directions for developing an evaluation, from articulating the purpose through reporting the results. It includes questions to consider in designing evaluations, sample instruments, analyses of methods and approaches, as well as discussion of the range and types of data that may be collected, useful models and theories of evaluation, multiple perspectives and contested issues. The monograph places the guiding principles and step-by-step approach within the context of the larger implications of implementing change at the individual and institutional level and offers a series of lessons learned to assist practitioners in thinking through the larger ramifications of evaluating diversity on college and university campuses. For the second monograph, the key audience — all those who need to play a role in persuading people that assessment is fundamentally about improving higher education — includes diversity practitioners, college and university administrators, and foundation and corporate funders.

Finally, the third volume, *A Diversity Research Agenda*, offers an overview of the existing research on diversity and calls for further research about the impact of diversity on higher education. New conceptions, frameworks, and approaches are needed as the field becomes more complex, and the failure to provide adequate evidence poses such grave policy and legal consequences. The volume identifies specific areas in the field of diversity research and assessment where more study is warranted. It also urges higher education institutions to encourage this kind of research and allocate more resources to support it. The key audience for the third monograph — all those who need to play a role in persuading people that assessment is fundamentally about improving higher education — includes diversity practitioners, college and university administrators, foundation and corporate funders, and those who will actually engage in assessment.

To Form a More Perfect Union in particular tries to do justice to this historic period of experimentation in higher education, one that evokes many of the same democratic aspirations undergirding our nation's founding. By deliberately dismantling some of the more egregious barriers to equal opportunity in higher education during this last half of the 20th century, the academy is indeed seeking, as the constitution's preamble boldly claims, "to establish Justice" and "promote the general Welfare." As the most diverse students in our nation's history come to campuses to work together, learn together, live together, this next saga in our nation's maturation unfolds. The academy has begun to embrace its civic role of educating students not simply to sit side by side but to foster "a more perfect union" in the face of and through the powerful insights of differences. That difficult, challenging task has taken root on our campuses. This volume examines what that new academy looks like, what people have learned along the way, and where higher education needs to go next in order to make good on our nation's promissory note.

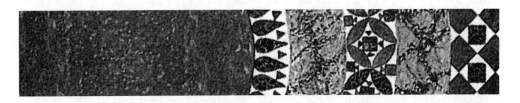

Acknowledgments

This monograph and the AAC&U project that generated it, "Understanding the Difference Diversity Makes: Assessing Campus Diversity Initiatives," was in every sense of the word a collaborative project. Its six diversity scholars worked together intensively over a three-year period, meeting, debating, editing each other's words, and refining each other's ideas. There were six funding agencies that supported this work, all of whom sent program officers to participate at various points in the planning and conceptual process.

The initial exploratory meeting brought program officers from the Lilly Endowment, the Philip Morris Companies Inc., the William and Flora Hewlett Foundation, and the Ford Foundation together one wintry February in 1995 in Ann Arbor, Michigan along with the group of evaluators serving as consultants to diversity programs at each philanthropic organization. We met periodically for over a year, expanding the group of funding agencies and representatives to discuss what insights our separate research offered, how those insights were refined when juxtaposed to one another, and how our findings might assist colleges and universities in their continuing commitment to diversity, excellence, and social responsibility.

Dr. Raymond Bacchetti, Program Officer at the William and Flora Hewlett Foundation, was especially engaged in this question having just launched their "Pluralism and Unity" initiative and has been a significant influence in conceptualizing and sustaining the project. He sharpened the edges of our conversations and his taut eloquence with words was a challenge to our writing collective. Kitty Breen, formerly Education Specialist from the Philip Morris Companies Inc., enlivened and warmed our exchanges, reminding us always that understanding how diversity works and doesn't work on campus matters deeply. Her colleague, Diane Eidman, Manager of the Domestic Violence Program at Philip Morris Companies Inc., gave continuity to the project. Sam Cargile, formerly Program Officer of the Lilly Endowment, was there from the very beginning pressing for more analysis, more comparisons, and evaluation language accessible to those not trained in the discipline. Ralph Lundgren of the Lilly Endowment honored Sam's involvement by contributing funds to the project after Sam's departure. Betty Overton-Adkins, Program Officer at the W.K. Kellogg Foundation, hosted one of our planning meetings before the project was a project and helped us craft a clearer purpose and clarify the context for our research. Carol Ramsey of the James Irvine Foundation joined later in the discussions but immediately understood the importance of the work and its congruence with initiatives at the Irvine Foundation. Author Hughes, also a Program Officer at the Irvine Foundation, helped shape our two California presidential roundtables in 1998 hosted each time at Irvine's headquarters.

Edgar Beckham, Program Officer for the Campus Diversity Initiative at the Ford Foundation, played a key leadership role throughout the project and was one of the most astute editors of our work. Insistent in prodding our thinking throughout the three-year process, he queried our findings, pushed at the edges of our initial conceptual certainties, and spurred us on with indefatigable enthusiasm. There wasn't a project meeting he missed and the prose in the text flows more smoothly because of his pen.

We are especially grateful to the five foundations and one corporate philanthropy for helping colleges and universities do a better job of turning diversity into an asset and equality and tolerance into more common campus practice. We thank the following for their support of this AAC&U evaluation project: The Ford Foundation, the William and Flora Hewlett Foundation, the James Irvine Foundation, the W. K. Kellogg Foundation, the Lilly Endowment, and the Philip Morris Companies Inc. They have helped higher education serve all of their students better and refine notions of what academic excellence actually is.

The staff at AAC&U supporting this project has been remarkable in its commitment, support, and high standards. Lee Harper, Program Associate for the first two thirds of the project, as rapporteur of our meetings, made our jumble of words sound coherent and, as project manager, made sure the papers and people flying about all over the country got to the right places at the right time. Brinton Ramsey, Program Associate for this last third of the project, plunged right in as if she had been part of the group from the beginning, adding her own expertise in evaluation to improve our thinking and our writing. Our Senior Editor, Bridget Puzon, made sure the manuscript met AAC&U's high standards, and Ann Kammerer lent her artistic eye to the design. Suzanne Hyers, Production Coordinator, made all the production machinery work against the odds, as usual.

Finally, we are grateful to the students, faculty, staff, and administrators at hundreds of campuses involved in the campus diversity initiatives at the core of this study. It is their insights, their reports, their candid assessments of their own projects, and their passionate commitment to equality and to education that was the inspiration for our work. We hope we have honored them well.

Caryn McTighe Musil, AAC&U
Mildred García, Arizona State University West
Cynthia A. Hudgins, University of Michigan
Michael T. Nettles, University of Michigan
William E. Sedlacek, University of Maryland
Daryl G. Smith, Claremont Graduate University

September 16, 1999

A Brief Historical Background

There is only one subject-matter for education, and that is Life in all its manifestations. (Alfred North Whitehead, *The Aims of Education*, in Levine 1998)

As the university becomes more open to and representative of the diverse peoples, experiences, traditions, and cultures that compose America, its impulse to find explanations for those parts of our history and our culture we have ignored grows proportionally. (Levine 1998)

I remember in my "Women in the Third World" class, one of the first things my professor talked about was embracing similarity in the heart of difference. And it took me so long to understand what she meant, and maybe I . . . just took [it] . . . my own way, but I felt . . . it was about . . . getting yourself out of your context somehow, or recognizing that you are in your context, and everything that you see, and everything that you believe has so much to do with . . . where you come from. (Musil 1992)

A. U.S. Engagement with Diversity: Founded in Pluralism

Diversity is not new to the United States. The richness of diversity and the problems of difference characterized the United States before it became a nation and continue today to be a source both of strength and contention. Diversity and the debate about its meaning and implementation are also not new to higher education. The examples we present do not presume to offer a full picture of this complex and persistent issue in higher education. Other scholarly books and institutional case histories abound. We will merely select a few historic details that punctuate the point.

Since the founding of the earliest institutions of higher learning in the United States—Harvard College (1636), the College of William and Mary (1693), and Yale University (1701)—the purposes and practices of colleges and universities have been expanded and altered in a dynamic relationship with the needs and demands of the nation. While some would have us believe that the contemporary engagement with diversity is orchestrated by a handful of academics who came of age in the political turmoil of the sixties, debates about diversity have existed in American higher education since the dawning of its existence. We have only to look to the nation's first college to see an example of one of those debates. Harvard's 1692 charter in effect abolished the Board of Overseers, thereby dissolving the Reformation pattern of joint secular-ecclesiastical college governance. The motivation for excluding government officials came from the fear felt by the college's Congregationalists that "a few Anglicans or even Baptists might obtain ex officio seats" (Herbst 1982). The College reformulated its governance structure, then, in response to a growing uneasiness about the increasing "denominational diversity."

A more contemporary example can be found in the evolution of the Michigan Union, the center of student organizations and activity at the University of Michigan which opened its doors in 1919. It was not until 1956, however, that women were officially allowed to enter the Union through the front doors or to enjoy all its facilities. The exclusionary rules were strictly enforced by a guard posted at the front doors (Port & Yachnin 1998).

Perhaps nowhere is the controversy about diversity clearer than in the national portrait of college students themselves. The face of higher education in the United States has changed over time as our nation gradually sought to make education available to more citizens. With the creation of women's colleges which began with Wesleyan College in the south and Mount Holyoke in the north, both chartered in 1836, and the creation of historically black colleges which began with Cheyney University of Pennsylvania in 1837, higher education began to extend educational opportunity to more students, albeit in segregated campus settings. The Morrill Federal Land Grant Act of 1862 expanded both the access to and purpose of higher education by extending opportunity for college to the children of "the industrial classes," to quote the legislation.

During the last half of the twentieth century, an even more dramatic change in the profile of higher education in the United States has occurred. In this period, campuses have committed themselves to fulfilling some of our nation's deepest democratic aspirations by engaging in a serious effort to educate the most genuinely diverse population of students ever. In the last five decades, a number of changes have dramatically altered the profile of colleges and universities in the United States. With the passage of the G.I. Bill after World War II, the opportunity to earn a college degree was extended to large segments of working-class Americans who in pre-war years had neither the financial means nor the national and local support to attend college. Consequently, higher education increased its population significantly. Among the veterans, there were many new groups who had been largely absent from earlier college classes; however, almost all of the new enrollees were male and the vast majority of them were white.

With the enactment of the Civil Rights Act of 1964, access to higher education expanded once more, this time to include Americans of color, most of whom had been systematically denied college entrance to the majority of institutions. The Act marked the official end of de jure racial segregation, thus creating the opportunity, for the first time, to develop racially inclusive student bodies. With the increases in enrollment of students of color throughout the 1960s and 1970s, higher education also witnessed an increase in civil rights activism and racial awareness. Horowitz (1987) refers to the "triggering experiences" of that era that brought students together across race. Such activities as sit-ins and freedom rides, and later, demands for ethnic studies programs and residential practices focused on race and ethnicity, brought racial issues onto campuses in the United States in a way not previously experienced.

Women as a defined group were the next new students who altered the traditional student-body profile. The number of women increased from 32 percent of undergraduates in 1950 to 55 percent today. Adding to the diversity, adult education that reached out to an older student population expanded significantly at the close of the 1960s, especially as a result of the G.I. Bill for Vietnam veterans, continuing education programs for women, and the expansion of community college systems. Since the 1965 Immigration Act (Hart-Celler Act), the number of students from Asia and Latin America has also increased measurably.

These events, combined with other changes in governmental and institutional policy over the last several decades, have dramatically increased overall enrollment in higher education at the same time that educational opportunity has been extended to new groups. In 1880, the total higher education enrollment was 156,756. By 1920 that number had increased to 597,880. By the fall semester of 1960, it had increased to 3,639,847 and by 1994, the total student enrollment catapulted to 14,304,803 (U.S. Department of Education 1997). Today, 28 percent of students are non-white, 55 percent are female, and 43 percent are students over the age of twenty-five. African-American enrollment, for example, increased at a faster rate between 1976 and 1994 than that of white students: 40.2 percent versus 14.8 percent (Nettles & Perna 1997). Latino enrollment has grown by 39.6 percent since 1990, and the 4.6 percent increase in Latino enrollment in 1995 was the largest one-year gain among the four major ethnic groups (Carter & Wilson 1997). Asian American enrollment has doubled since 1980 with the largest growth at four-year institutions (Carter & Wilson 1997). Asian American enrollment accounted for nearly 5 percent of the total enrollment at colleges and universities in 1992 (U.S. Department of Education 1995). International student enrollment in 1996-97 was at a record high with 457,984 students (Desruisseaux 1997). Despite such impressive growth in enrollment, students of color, except for Asian American students, continue to be underrepresented in higher education relative to their representation in the college-age population.

The profile of students in higher education has changed not only by race, sex, and age, but also by socioeconomic background. Even by the middle of the current century, the typical college student came from a wealthier family than most other Americans. In the 1960s, for example, the median family income of students was almost twice as high as the national median income (Dey & Hurtado 1994). Over the decades, that economic distinction has begun to blur as today's college students span a much wider variety of economic backgrounds.

Just as the demographics of higher education have changed to more accurately mirror the demographics of American society, so too has the curriculum. During the last three decades, in particular, our understanding of epistemology, academic disciplines and their methodologies has been altered. Parallel to and, in many cases, intertwined with the dramatic expansion of undergraduate students, the scholarship upon which knowledge is constructed underwent a dramatic change. With the new scholarship by and about formerly neglected groups, an intellectual resurgence has invigorated academic disciplines, disrupting former ways of understanding, and challenging higher education to rethink what it teaches, the way it teaches, and why it teaches what it does.

We find ourselves at a moment in United States history where the questions of historic inequalities and continued patterns of discrimination have become part of our national conversation. At this moment, there is an urgency to move from talk to action, and our collective response has profound societal implications. At no other time in history has the enrollment of colleges and universities in the United States been as diverse as it is today. Higher education is therefore unequivocally at the center of the debate about diversity. The academy has the opportunity to provide leadership to the nation on how it will address past legacies and how it will proceed into the next century.

B.   The Evolving Understanding of Diversity

Historically, colleges and universities have always assumed a certain commitment to diversity, and the academy in general has typically embraced diversity as a necessary component of intellectual inquiry. What distinguishes the current moment in time is the more widespread exploration of diversity in the context of power, injustice, and social responsibility. Our colleges today have diversified their student bodies in part as a response to the larger political movements in the sixties and seventies which called on the nation to honor its democratic principles of equality, opportunity, and mutual well-being. In addition to a call for altering prejudiced attitudes, there was an insistence that we grapple with persistent patterns of inequality.

To do that effectively, academic institutions are realizing that the changes will involve more than a shift in the national student demographic profile. It will involve even more than hiring a more diverse faculty, administration, and staff. It will require a rethinking of the purposes and practices of the academy itself. Daryl G. Smith has offered a useful model discussed in more detail later in the monograph which suggests the range of ways institutions can think about what diversity means and what it can contribute to institutional vitality and educational excellence (Smith 1995). Smith refers to four key dimensions of campus diversity: (1) access and success, (2) climate and intergroup relations, (3) education and scholarship, and (4) institutional vitality and viability (see chart, page 40).

Emerging understandings about diversity and higher education have evolved from the remarkable experimentation on campuses in a wide variety of diversity programs, focused especially on the first three of Smith's dimensions. The richest diversity initiatives with the strongest impact have moved far beyond the question of access, while never losing sight of its centrality. Colleges and universities are paying more attention to how well new student populations succeed and how effectively institutions welcome faculty, administrators, and staff from underrepresented groups. They are also recognizing the influence of campus climate and intergroup relations on retention and responding with innovative programs. They are examining traditional structures and practices that have created barriers to a diverse student population. And they are encouraging new scholarship about formerly ignored groups and issues, thus adding to and revising the knowledge base of our disciplines, stimulating innovations in curriculum, and bringing renewed attention to improving teaching and learning.

Our understanding of diversity is also evolving. The framework for understanding the meaning of diversity has become more complex. Most people understand that not all differences are neutral. Some differences mark people positively or negatively. Above all, no one is defined or lives in the world in a single identity category, but rather in multiple roles: through racial identities and gendered ones; through religious affiliations and ethnic legacies; through socioeconomic attributes and sexual orientations. Each of us both inherits identities through our cultural roots and affiliates with new communities throughout our lives. We are always members of many different communities, some in conflict with one another, and our daily task is to mediate among the various communities we inhabit. We also understand now that these differences are fluid and contextual, not static. One or the other of our identities may be more or less salient in different contexts, and we move between our identities as we adjust to these varied contexts.

The new operational framework of diversity respects and embraces this complexity. Without it, we risk creating bad admissions policies, inadequate counseling services, faulty knowledge, and an institutional identity that suppresses the rich possibilities within its reach.

Fewer people are settling for diversity as a mere matter of numerical calculation on a federal form. Instead, diversity is understood today as a means of embracing values that promote the common good. Diversity prompts us to develop new capacities to cross boundaries, to connect through differences, and, in so doing, to discover what we share in common as human beings. Instead of acquiescing to a campus where people function in parallel and passive pluralism, the challenge before us is to foster engaged, relational pluralism. By doing that, we knit our otherwise fragmented identities into a whole even as we knit our fractured communities.

Engaging across differences, especially in an academic institution, must involve more than personal interactions. It requires knowledge. The academy is ideally suited to enhance the knowledge—historical, cultural, sociological, psychological, aesthetic—we need about one another and ourselves, and to embed that knowledge in the curriculum and co-curriculum. Some of that knowledge is painful and shameful, disputed and debated, emerging and isolated. It is knowledge as one person put it, "inconvenient for us to know," for it can challenge assumptions and make us question the adequacy or veracity of what we have been taught. Engaging such intellectual inquiries, however, preserves academic integrity. Avoiding it perpetuates misunderstandings, misrepresentations, and faulty thinking.

As the operational framework for diversity has broadened and become more complex over the past three decades, it has become an increasingly essential component of institutional mission, expressing an institution's highest obligations to itself and its students, and to a world lived in common with others.

2

Centrality of Diversity to the Academy's Educational Mission

"Diversity. Philip Morris' competitive edge," says an advertisement for the Philip Morris Companies Inc. "A healthy mix. That's the only kind there is," reads the advertisement for Blue Cross Blue Shield. "Driving our work force diversity is our fundamental belief that valuing differences—among employees, customers, shareowners, suppliers, and the communities in which we live and work—is a business and moral imperative," writes Rockwell International Corporation (Hilliard-Jones 1996). A highly visible Cotton Incorporated television advertising campaign spotlights a group of young children of different races emerging from a subway. The voice-over tells us, "What's the very first thing we need to know? That we won't get anywhere if we don't get there together."

Diversity. It is in TV commercials, on the menus in restaurants, visible in fashions, rock music, and neighborhoods. Pews in churches and rows in movie theaters have been altered to accommodate wheel chairs. While English is our common national language, it is not the only language spoken by Americans. A woman today can now realistically aspire to be Secretary of State as well as a secretary. Ramadan draws hundreds of worshipers to the Islamic Temple in Washington, D.C., and forty minutes away, a Buddhist temple has been established in an affluent county in Virginia where fox hunting is still a popular sport.

A.   Principal Arguments for Addressing Diversity

As pervasive as diversity is in American culture today, there are some who see diversity as a distraction from more important issues, as a threat to national unity and local communities, or as a collection of special interest groups. In the context of higher education, such criticism has led to heated debates over the content of the curriculum, resistance by some to programs specifically designed to attract or support populations newly included at colleges and universities, and an insistence that focusing on particularities of one's identity group is, at best, irrelevant or at worst, divisive. Some people worry that only difference is valued, not commonalities. They see groups cluster together and fear disunity will be the consequence. So much new scholarship has been generated that some fear that what they regard as classic traditions will be lost. Others believe minorities or women get unwarranted special privileges at the expense of more qualified people. A portion are convinced we have gone too far in accommodating new populations on campuses and sacrificed excellence in the process.

Even those who want to eliminate discrimination and open up opportunities in higher education for underrepresented groups are in a quandary. Diversity is not simple but complex. There is, for instance, increasing confusion about racial categories. For example, the single box choices in past census forms are inadequate to capture the growing number of people who are biracial or multiracial. While Asian Americans, as a group, lead whites in percentage of bachelor's degrees, the 1990 U.S. Census revealed that 63.1 percent of today's Asian-American population was born in a country other than the United States (Carter & Wilson 1997), and, when disaggregated by national and ethnic group, many Asian-American students from new immigrant populations need academic support programs (Hune 1998). Economic differences within a single racial category as well as between racial groups confuse these categories even more. How can remedies for discrimination be created in such a context? Many are uncertain about how to proceed.

As people more freely hold on to their cultural, racial, or religious identities, the differences between people become less submerged, and more palpable. How to navigate a course in the midst of such a heterogeneous world is a new challenge for many, especially those who formerly were able to take their particular identities and affiliations for granted as a norm that others would seek to imitate or, at least, never challenge. Many are tentatively feeling their way in a world where multiplicity is the norm. The process has predictably not been without discomfort, misunderstandings, and bewilderment. It has also been characterized, however, by a sense of excitement, enrichment, and dazzling possibilities.

The fiercest critics of diversity have capitalized on bewilderment and unease. Their most vocal opposition has been waged in the public arena far outside the boundaries of the academy with their greatest impact on legal court cases and public referendums.

These, in turn, have serious consequences for campus policies and practices, especially in admissions, financial aid, and support programs. Despite troubling policy setbacks, the public at large and higher education as a sector have embraced diversity rather than run for cover in the face of it. They understand that diversity, like the air we breathe, is a given in our lives.

In a 1998 national poll (DYG, Inc. 1998), for instance, 65 percent of Americans judged that colleges are not doing a good job if their graduates cannot get along in a diverse population. Although 58 percent believe the nation is growing apart, 71 percent think diversity education helps bring people together. Two-thirds believe colleges should require students to take at least one cultural and ethnic diversity course to graduate. Despite setbacks for affirmative action in the courts, 66 percent of those polled think colleges should take explicit steps to ensure diversity in the student body, and 75 percent support similar steps in faculty representation.

If diversity is the norm and will continue to be so, higher education has a special role to play, the public believes, in ensuring that such differences become sources of strength, that is, a resource rather than a problem. The academy, therefore, offers a powerful laboratory for defining new democratic practices of equality, opportunity, and inclusion. For the most part it has taken on the challenge, motivated by a series of compelling arguments that it should do no less. These arguments include the academic, moral, civic, demographic and economic arguments.

Academic argument

In the academy's most recent iteration of its long engagement with diversity, several arguments have persuaded the majority of institutions to begin to re-evaluate campus practices and policies in order to foster deeper learning, create more inclusive communities, and prepare students to assume full responsibilities for sustaining a diverse and robust democratic society. It is no surprise that the most influential argument to the higher education community is an academic one. Many believe diversity is deeply linked to insuring academic excellence. Imbued with the conviction that scholarship is enhanced by multiple viewpoints, academicians have increasingly recognized that knowledge suffers when differing perspectives are ignored.

Over the last three decades, as the engagement with diversity became more intentional and sustained, new insights about diversity and learning have evolved. The most compelling of those insights is the recognition that diversity is essential for excellence. Through diversity, the knowledge base that serves as the foundation of the academy becomes richer, more accurate, and more nuanced. Diversity also encourages a deeper understanding of students and the ways in which their complex and dynamic identities influence what they learn and how they learn it. In these ways diversity drives higher education toward excellence in teaching and learning.

Moral argument

A second argument that has motivated many in the academy to support diversity is a moral one. Many support diversity because they believe it is simply the right thing to do. It directs our attention to the nation's unfinished business. A commitment to diversity is seen as a commitment to equality and equal opportunity. Part of the moral argument is the recognition that historical inequalities have produced current inequalities. Few argue there is a level playing field, and are, as a consequence, reluctant to create policies that assume there is one. Most assume that to do so would perpetuate injustice rather than re-establish fairness.

Civic argument

Closely related to the moral argument is a civic one. Based on the belief in the civic importance of an educated citizenry, democracy depends on the meaningful participation and practice of deliberative dialogue among its peoples with the corollary that citizen responsibility is an essential infrastructure in a democratic society. Democracy's integrity and stability depend on making certain that the communities people live in are fair and just. Higher education's unique national task is preparing people, through college experience, to be responsible members of their communities, graduating from college with a greater sense of obligation to the well-being of the whole.

Demographic argument

The fifth compelling argument for addressing diversity rests on simple mathematics. Colleges understand that they need to educate current and projected generations of college students, the majority of whom are female, nearly 30 percent of whom are students of color, 40 percent of whom are older adults, and nearly half of whom are first-generation college students. Heterogeneity is projected to be the norm in the future. By the year 2010, for instance, demographers (Hodgkinson 1992) looking at race alone predict that eleven states and the District of Columbia will have significant minority youth populations. Furthermore, approximately half of those seventeen and younger will live in these eleven states. Higher education has, in many instances, been a catalyst mirroring these changing demographics in student populations. It therefore has a powerful motive for creating an educational environment in which current and future students can thrive.

Economic argument

The demographic argument is tied to another compelling reason for making diversity integral to the academy. It is a matter of economic opportunity and economic justice. Research indicates that educational attainment of the family head is directly related to the income and living standards of the family. The higher the educational attainment, the higher the income. Those who do not have higher education degrees face low and declining living standards with little prospect for improving their economic standing (Mortenson Research Seminar October 97). Poverty threatens democracy, and of those who are poor, a disproportionate number are women, children, and people of color. It is in the nation's long-range economic interest to invest in educating those who until recent decades have been left out of the academy.

The economic structure of society also calls for a skilled work force. Part of higher education's mission has historically been to produce the country's professional work force. The current work force is already part of a global economy, interdependent and intertwined with the rest of the world in ways unimagined before World War II. The projected majority of entry-level workers in the United States work force in the year 2000 will be white women and women and men of color, which means that today's educated student must have skills to motivate, understand, market to, listen to, and learn from a multicultural environment. If college students are not educated to excel in and shape such a world, they will have been deprived of a substantial educational advantage.

The nation's most enlightened corporate leaders also want workers who not only function well in and value diversity, but know how to make it benefit themselves and their communities. Economic investments and dividends, then, are understood in a much broader way. In a 1998 survey of business leaders in the state of Washington, 84 percent said it was important for colleges to prepare graduates to function in a more diverse work force. Three quarters of these business leaders believe diversity education brings society together (Elway Research 1998). Students need a new, more intentional, kind of education that helps them know who they are, gives them an opportunity to learn more about others, and exposes them to the interplay of multiple perspectives. Providing experience in collaboration, this new education expands their view of the world. As students and as citizens, they can then understand how diversity—well deployed and creatively exploited—benefits them and benefits society.

B.   Campuses as Laboratories

Moved by such arguments for diversity, institutions of higher education have collectively implemented diversity interventions in nearly every dimension of institutional life, from curriculum to faculty development, from campus climate to institutional leadership to connections with the community.

Campuses are becoming aware that they offer what most residential neighborhoods in the United States do not: shared space where students encounter more diversity than they ever could at home. Given the economic, racial, and ethnic stratification of our neighborhoods and schools, college campuses frequently are the multivalent space bringing people from all kinds of backgrounds into potential relationship with one another. A campus is, in that sense, a laboratory. As a laboratory, it offers students and those who work at colleges and universities the opportunity to develop new capacities for learning across differences.

Increasingly people on campuses realize they could potentially create a new kind of cross-cultural and intercultural learning community in which everyone has a voice and everyone matters, everyone teaches and everyone learns. Initially, many were under the mistaken notion that simply bringing diverse populations to a given campus would be sufficient. With time and experience, more people understand the challenge differently. Diversity of numbers is not enough. The deeper challenge is to help people see themselves in relation to one another, what AAC&U has referred to as "relational pluralism." The goal is to achieve what John Dewey called capacities for associated living (Dewey 1927). To achieve such capacities requires continuing practice—in the classroom, the campus community, and the wider community, as we learn how to move from what Mary Louise Pratt calls "the comfort zone" into "the contact zone . . . the space in which people geographically and historically separated come into contact with each other and establish ongoing relations" (Pratt 1990).

To make such interactions enhance learning and build a sense of community involves acquiring new knowledge and cultivating new attitudes of mind and heart. Among the qualities needed are respect, recognition, and deliberative dialogue among participants with equal standing, the ability to engage difference without erasing it, and the realization that because each person has partial knowledge, other people's perspectives are needed in order to more fully know the truth. Finally, each one needs to confront difficult issues about justice and inequalities, both present and past. If higher education cultivates such social and intellectual capacities in its graduates, the phrase *e pluribus unum* will be more than an aspiration, and the concept of global community more than a TV commercial for IBM computers.

3

The Emerging Diversity Mosaic

In a small Midwestern college where students come primarily from Norwegian farming families, first-year students compare the experiences of African Americans, Chinese Americans, and Norwegian Americans in their freshman core courses. One young woman says, "This course expanded my horizons and introduced me to worlds I would have never known otherwise."

Located in the heart of the Old Confederacy where at the end of the twentieth century the city was fractured by a proposal to put a statue of Arthur Ashe next to the row of Confederate generals, a university has, by its own determined, patient partnership with the community, become the seat of the most comprehensive archival collections about the African American community in that city before World War II.

An English professor in a faculty development summer seminar on gender and literature said with unabashed pleasure, "Because I learned how to do a gender analysis of literature, I just doubled everything I can teach!"

A Reader's Theater performance at an elite private school presented a play written and performed by service employees and students. It provided a rare opportunity for the employees to express who they are, what they do, and what they want from life. A literary magazine, Punching the Clock, *was written and edited by service employees.*

These vignettes are but a hint of the range of experimentation taking place on college campuses today. They suggest something about the personal and institutional transformation possible when diversity is claimed as an educational and societal asset. They also point to one of the conundrums in trying to assess the impact of diversity on campuses in the United States today. The institutional redesign is an evolving one, very much in the act of creation. It resembles an emerging mosaic. Mosaic is a common metaphor in the literature of diversity in which individual pieces or distinctive identities, as in particular pieces of glass or stone in a mosaic, need not erase their particularity in order to simultaneously contribute to a larger picture. In fact, the whole assumes its recognizable design because the individual pieces have been placed in exact but utterly distinctive relationship to the whole and to the other individual pieces. Mosaic also captures the emerging narrative of diversity at this juncture in time: the story of a single effort here, a cluster of similar efforts there, and a multi-dimensional approach elsewhere. No one institution offers a finished work of art. Only by placing the individual institutional stories of progress, missteps, and lessons learned in relationship to one another does a fuller, more accurate, national mosaic emerge.

Seeing this emerging mosaic is tricky. While it surfaces in both everyday and extraordinary changes, many of them are accompanied by discomfort, exhilaration, contestation, consensus, renewed optimism, and rekindled cynicism. It is clearly a work in progress, but one that many hands are assembling. This chapter seeks to describe that process of construction.

Five foundations and one corporate philanthropy have been instrumental in supporting colleges and universities who have chosen to undertake this work. Diversity initiatives generated by their grant recipients form the core of this study. The nature of the grants has therefore influenced the kind of diversity program evaluated in this monograph. The reader will find, for example, very little on recruitment and admissions but quite a lot on curriculum, climate, and institutional change.

To assist institutions as they sought to incorporate diversity into campus life, the five foundations and one corporate philanthropy central to this study invested in four principal areas: curriculum, faculty development, campus climate, and public education. Three secondary areas also surfaced but with far less attention: campus/community connections; student-centered projects; and research and resource materials. The sponsoring agencies below are listed chronologically according to the year they launched their major diversity initiatives. (See the Appendix for the roster of grantees.)

The James Irvine Foundation worked exclusively with California schools. Making grants to twenty-two private, four-year institutions over a ten-year period beginning in 1987, Irvine's primary goal was to admit and graduate greater numbers of underrepresented populations in California. About one-third of their grants were awarded to diversify the curriculum as a means of retaining students of color. A larger proportion of the grants supported financial aid awards, additional staff to recruit underrepresented students, bridge programs to college, new student support services, and outreach programs to the local communities. The foundation also awarded grants to six schools for recruitment of more diverse faculty and to another six for projects that fostered research and collaboration between faculty and students, both graduate and undergraduate.

The Ford Foundation formally announced its Campus Diversity Initiative in February 1990. In a letter signed by seven college and university presidents, the director of the American Council on Education's Office of Minority Concerns, the president of the College Board, and the president of the Ford Foundation, the Foundation challenged higher education "to embrace the rich diversity of American life in a manner that enhances the educational experiences of all students."

Between 1990 and 1999, the foundation either directly or indirectly assisted 294 colleges and universities through its Campus Diversity Initiative, some through direct grants, others through intermediary organizations such as the Washington Center for Improving the Quality of Undergraduate Education. The Center then assisted forty-six institutions in Washington State. The Association of American Colleges and Universities was another intermediary organization involving 148 institutions across the country. While a few grants supported resource development and student-oriented projects, most Ford Foundation funding was focused on faculty development and curricular innovation. A cluster of grants through AAC&U also fostered campus-community connections through "Community Seminars" and "Racial Legacies and Learning." The foundation also invested in a Public Information Project on campus diversity that sought to inform the concerned public about the positive ways in which colleges and universities were responding to diversity and about the societal benefits of such work. The foundation encouraged its grantees to define diversity very broadly and to address the intersections of race, class, gender, ethnicity, religion, and sexual orientation.

The Lilly Endowment diversity initiative was more singularly focused on race. Called "Improving Racial and Ethnic Diversity and Campus Climate at Four-Year Independent Midwest Colleges," it awarded grants to forty institutions in eight Midwestern states, from 1991 to 1994. The goal was to enhance racial and ethnic diversity, build more inclusive communities, improve campus climate, foster understanding and appreciation of differences among members of the campus community, and ultimately, as a result of those changes, to graduate students of color in greater numbers, with a greater sense of personal fulfillment and more graduate and career options open to them. A significant number of schools focused on curriculum revision, fewer on faculty development, and a large number on campus climate through a significant investment in co-curricular programs.

In 1992, the *Philip Morris Companies Inc.* announced a three-year grant initiative, "Tolerance on Campus: Establishing Common Ground," which made awards to eleven four-year colleges and universities. The goal of the initiative was to help campuses improve race relations and to create stronger communities of civility and respect. The grants supported a wide variety of projects, including both co-curricular and curricular programming. Some of the campuses emphasized curricular transformation and faculty development while others focused upon resource development, workshops, and peer education programs. Campuses invested in a wide-range of innovative diversity initiatives. The main focus of the projects was on increasing awareness and knowledge of different groups on campus and improving relations between the campus and the local community.

The William and Flora Hewlett Foundation initiative also drew attention to the relationship of diversity and community as the focus for their grantees. In their "Pluralism and Unity" initiative, begun in 1994, the Foundation has awarded fifty-two grants over the past five years. Hewlett's initiative seeks to encourage campuses to engage pluralism and campus community simultaneously, supporting actions that advance the development of colleges and universities as places where students build dynamic connections between themselves and various communities. Campus initiatives differed widely and included institution-building activities across departments, curricular transformation, student affairs, and faculty development. The main focus of these initiatives was to support colleges and universities in building the creative capacity for effective citizenship across diverse communities.

In 1994, the *W. K. Kellogg Foundation* launched its Centers of Excellence Initiative for Historically Black Colleges. In this initiative, the Kellogg Foundation worked only with historically black colleges and universities, investing significantly in ten institutions that defined an area on their campus where they wanted to develop a center of excellence. The ten grants of three million dollars each enabled the institution to determine the nature of its center. Kellogg's focus, like the Ford Foundation's, was ultimately on the production of knowledge more than on campus climate. However, the foundation viewed these grants as contributing to the diversity of students in United States higher education.

As part of the Kellogg Foundation's Higher Education strategic plan, the initiative that started with Historically Black Colleges and Universities has been expanded to the Native American Higher Education Initiative and one focused on Hispanic-Serving Institutions. In addition, the Kellogg Foundation has a Capitalizing on Diversity Steering Committee that reviews and funds programs that specifically address how best to capitalize on diversity in different environments including colleges and academic centers within institutions.

Taken together, the six funding agencies reflect the profile of campus-based diversity initiatives in the nation at large. While external funding certainly influences the focus, speed, and general acceptance of diversity initiatives, the vast majority of institutions in the United States have taken similar initiatives through their own institutional resources, motivated by educational, intellectual, and moral imperatives and by societal demands.

In the 1960s and 1970s institutions concentrated on access, especially for people of color, women as a group, and adult students. The 1980s and 1990s have been marked by a new set of questions. While access, retention, and graduation rates continue to be a concern, institutions now are using diversity as a resource for providing an educational environment in which *all* students thrive, intellectually and personally. There has been, therefore, a second wave of innovation, experimentation, and institutional self-evaluation putting diversity more squarely at the center of educational missions. Below are eight noticeable trends emerging from this later period of intense activity.

A.   Trends Across Campuses

Trends

1. From access to wide-ranging campus innovations
2. Movement toward creating more comprehensive plans
3. Emergence of new structures to coordinate diversity initiatives
4. Race as more than black and white
5. Diversity as more than race
6. From single to multiple and intersecting differences
7. From "fixing" new students to recasting institutional mission
8. Diversity as a catalyst for institutional improvement

1. From access to wide-ranging campus innovations

The cutting edge of diversity activity in the sixties and early seventies was the almost single-minded focus on making higher education accessible to students previously excluded by unfair laws and practices. The driving force in the late seventies and early eighties was on making the climate more welcoming to those new students, which included among other things the establishment of special studies like Black Studies, Puerto Rican and Chicano Studies, American Indian Studies, Asian American Studies, and women's studies. The eighties was distinguished by integrating that new scholarship into mainstream departmental courses, altering many of the traditional disciplines in the process. In the nineties, however, what had been mere wedges of change earlier on at only a representative number of campuses has become commonplace almost everywhere.

The first thing one notices on almost every campus is just how much activity is going on. The second thing is how varied those activities are. There is hardly a university or college that has not included diversity somewhere as part of its educational responsibilities. To do that, each institution has typically grappled with defining what diversity might mean on a given campus at a particular moment in time: Christians and students of color at Brandeis, women at Yale, African Americans at the University of Mississippi, international students at Luther College, gay and lesbian students at Northeastern University, disabled students at the University of Maryland, Chicano students at UCLA. There is also hardly an aspect of institutional life that has not somewhere been touched by a new attentiveness to diversity: the curriculum, student support services, admissions, athletics, residence life, alumni giving, governing boards, hiring, promotion, and tenure, and relations with the community outside the academy's wall. Few institutions have tackled all areas at once. The process is very much a work in progress, but a new academy is definitely under construction.

2. Movement toward creating more comprehensive plans

At some campuses where there has been such varied activity and at other campuses that are just getting started and want to set new programs in motion in a more coordinated way, a trend is emerging toward creating more comprehensive diversity plans. The Western Interstate Commission for Higher Education sponsored through its Diversity Institute a program in which its staff worked with institutions in twenty western states to create comprehensive diversity plans. The investment is heavy in the beginning of such work which involves collecting data for institutional audits of its current state in a wide range of campus areas, meeting consistently over time with a representative number of institutional leaders, and creating a campus-wide strategic plan as the culminating activity. President Everett Frost of Eastern New Mexico University believed the effort well worth it because a comprehensive plan set an institution-wide agenda owned by a wide range of campus leaders. Large midwestern universities like the University of Michigan adopted its encompassing Michigan Mandate on Diversity and New Agenda for Women, allocating resources, clarifying goals, and embedding evaluation into activities. Smaller institutions like Loyola College in Maryland used a grass roots approach appropriate for its smaller size with impressive involvement of faculty and staff on committees to formulate its Curriculum Infusion Program and drawing deeply on its Catholic tradition of justice as a rationale for its engagement with diversity. The challenge of overarching plans is to ensure that once resources are aligned with the goals, there is a translation from plan to practice, and that progress is monitored on a regular basis.

3. Emergence of new structures to coordinate diversity initiatives

On an increasing number of campuses where there have been significant amounts of diversity initiatives, institutions have begun to create new structures to coordinate some or all of those activities. Sometimes it is a committee, like the Diversity Action Council at the University of Arizona, formed as an advisory group to the president, which over-sees the coordination and integration of diversity into curricular, co-curricular, and institution-wide policy initiatives on campus. Other times it is a new appointment, like the Associate Vice President for Multicultural Affairs at the University of Minnesota or the Special Assistant to the President for Multicultural and Community Affairs at Ferris State, each position having been allocated new resources and a portfolio with coordina-tion of diversity activities as a major part of the job description. The University of Maryland has the Diversity Accountability and Implementation Plan, a fully institution-alized, campus-wide program that provides institutional stability for diversity planning. What typically distinguishes such committees or structures from others on campus is the cross-divisional perspectives and incentive to cooperate across the separate campus areas which have a tradition of operating autonomously. Among the issues of the new struc-tures are their authority, resources, and long-term individual value to those who partici-pate in them, especially faculty members because of the narrow reward structure of most promotion and tenure committees and the insularity of many academic departments.

4. Race as more than black and white

Legally sanctioned and culturally practiced patterns of race discrimination against African Americans, Asian American, Latino/Latinas, and American Indians have been a shameful part of higher education's history. Although all four racial minority groups have long histories, each seeking to resist these inequities in a variety of ways across time, the Civil Rights movement of the 1950s and 1960s was the most visible, dramatic, and successful in ultimately dismantling the most egregious racist policies and laws. In 1961, most Americans were riveted to the television broadcast of Governor George Wallace defying National Guard troops as he barred the entrance of two black students, Vivian Malone and James Hood, trying to register at the University of Alabama. At that time, African Americans were also the largest racial minority in the country, accounting for a greater total percentage of the population than the other three racial groups put together. While African Americans continue to be the largest racial minority today at 12.7 percent, the other groups have grown considerably and now total together 15.8 per-cent of the population (U.S. Bureau of the Census 1998). For most white Americans, and for many African Americans, however, the defining moment of the sixties, preceded by more than two hundred years of slavery, etched the racial struggle in the United States as a black-white conflict.

With the passage of the Civil Rights Act of 1964, a new era began in U.S. history. The power of the political movement for equality, coupled with the power of law and legislation, gave greater clout to other racial groups as they organized to claim their due as Americans. Higher education was a major arena in which those claims were tested. Non-black racial minorities began to be more visible and organized on campus. With new immigration waves from Central and South America and Asia following the 1965 U.S. Immigration Act and the 1986 Immigration Reform and Control Act, the racial complexion of the United States began to change overall. Asian Americans quadrupled their numbers between 1964 and 1998 (Carter & Wilson 1997), and Hispanics grew from 6.4 percent of the U.S. population in 1980 to 11.4 percent in 1998 (U.S. Bureau of the Census 1998). Campuses in the nineties are testimony to those changes, many of them reflecting geographic demography. UCLA no longer has a majority racial population, but Asian Americans are the largest racial group. While the Latino/Latina student enrollment is rising overall, it continues to vary in composition. At Southwest Texas State University, Chicano/Chicana students are more visible, but at Hostos Community College, Puerto Ricans are a critical mass, and at Florida Atlantic University Cuban Americans are more typical. For all these reasons, the older black-white paradigm is insufficient and misleading if one is seeking to understand race on today's college campuses or in today's communities. The issue is complicated by new evidence of tensions between communities of color, such as the black/Asian tensions that emerged during the nineties in Los Angeles and New York City. The complexity of the issue is also evidenced by the intergroup tensions of the different Latino/Latina populations, black populations and the Asian populations. A new interest in and acknowledgment of bi-racial and multi-racial identity has recently manifested itself among students on a number of campuses and is measurable in new scholarship being produced. The backlash by a vocal minority of whites who feel disenfranchised and discriminated against has added yet another difficult dynamic to campus and community relations. Creating fair racial policies and an educational environment, with race not an area for contestation but a resource in America's much more complicated racial mosaic, is the challenge to the academy as the century comes to a close. As W.E.B. DuBois said of the twentieth century, the problem of the twenty-first century may also be the problem of the color line. It's simply a far more complex series of lines than ever before.

5. Diversity as more than race

If the Civil Rights bill of 1964 unleashed new activism and attentiveness to all of the racial minorities in the United States, it also unleashed far more. The Civil Rights Act of 1964 made it unlawful to discriminate on the basis not only of color or race but on the basis of religion, sex, or national origin. The women's movement, which had already been given a boost by President Kennedy's Commission on Women in 1963, was the first large group ready to organize for equality inside and outside of the academy. New legislation forbidding sex discrimination in pay and employment in the late sixties followed in the early seventies by Title IX, affecting most areas in higher education, blended with a grass roots movement that eventually contributed to the new majority women now hold among college students. Activism on campus, the emergence of women's studies as a discipline, new campus structures like Women's Commissions and Title IX officers contributed to the architecture of the emerging new academy. Against this backdrop of activism, gays and lesbians, disabled people, and some religious groups began to forge new groupings, altering policies and opening up the curriculum in yet new ways. On some campuses, diversity still translates as race, but the trend nationally is toward recognizing the broad array of different cultural, religious, racial, national, and economic identities found on any given campus. The term diversity, in fact, came into existence largely because race or gender or sexual identity would no longer serve to adequately describe this expanded understanding, and diversity was, in turn, reflected in the legislation being passed and the scholarship being produced.

6. From single to multiple and intersecting differences

If for several decades each identity group forged its political agenda and helped dismantle inequality by distinguishing itself from other groups, by the nineties those differentiations were understood in far more complex ways. Initially there was often an inclination to claim one identity—as a Chicano, a woman, or a gay; during the mid-1980s and 1990s people increasingly shed simplistic notions of membership in a single undifferentiated category. Multiple and overlapping differences have replaced single and separate ones. It is now, for instance, more routinely understood that race is inflected by gender, that Latinos/Latinas come from diverse socioeconomic backgrounds, that Jews are found in all racial groups, that sexual orientation intersects all the other lines of difference, and that increasing numbers of students assign themselves to "mixed" racial, religious, and ethnic backgrounds. This shift has influenced intellectual theory, led to new areas of scholarly investigation, generated new courses, and made new alliances across disciplinary and personal boundaries possible. Nonetheless, constructing programming and curriculum, accounting for climate and access, and designing hiring policies to take into account such new understandings of diversity pose far more demanding challenges than they did decades ago. The challenge, however, also reflects more accurately the realities of people's lives as well as human history and culture.

7. From "fixing" new students to recasting institutional mission

Institutions are tackling such complexity more thoughtfully and consistently than ever before. There is evidence, too, that institutions are developing new capacities to engage issues of diversity in productive ways, although the pathway is sometimes bumpy and seldom a straight line. A growing number of institutions realize that diversifying students is only the beginning of a longer, more complex process. Instead of the model of "fixing" the "new, diverse student" to fit into an existing educational mold, more and more colleges and universities are taking a hard, critical look at the kind of learning environments into which students are being invited.

There is a mounting tendency, therefore, towards thinking of diversity in the larger framework of institutional context and mission. Rather than focusing exclusively on the diverse student as the add-on, institutions are rethinking their fundamental educational and societal purposes. Many institutions are increasingly attending to their capacities for educating diverse students to function in a diverse and interdependent global society. The agenda for diversity, then, has become more firmly rooted in the institution's overall mission rather than being a mandate to serve particular populations. Deeply connected to this major shift is the recognition that understanding diversity, negotiating diversity, taking grounded stands in the face of differences is of benefit to *all* students.

8. Diversity as a catalyst for institutional improvement

Another noticeable trend shows that diversity initiatives generate unexpected educational benefits for the institution as a whole. Among the forty institutions funded by the Lilly Endowment, the unanticipated consequences of the diversity grants were dramatic. One institution created a certificate program in multicultural studies. Another produced a new publication on multicultural arts programming. Still another gave awards to the best campus multicultural program. Throughout the group of forty, new multicultural clubs and resource centers were established. The excitement over faculty development initiatives in diversity also led to the creation of a faculty development center, overall improvements in pedagogy, instituting peer advising for all students, and the institution of peer counseling and expanded mentoring for all students. It also resulted in the establishment of tutoring and mentoring programs between a college and local schools, to minority alumni networks, and to a new interest on the part of student government in addressing diversity issues.

At a number of institutions funded by Lilly, there was evidence that such initiatives contributed to students of color feeling more comfortable and assuming more leadership roles and greater prominence on campus. However, there was occasionally some backlash from students who resented the attention other groups were getting, and frequently there was some resistance from the faculty. But the overall impact was positive. One professor expressed the sense of new possibilities, however vulnerable, "Certainly our grant has been a solid foundation on which to build . . . but our real success will be measured by our ability to translate the tough discussions into action, supported judiciously with finite resources, in positive and lasting ways in the years to come" (Sedlacek 1995).

A similar example is the Philip Morris Companies Inc. project at Duke University, where a President's Common Ground Fund was established to make small grants available for faculty, administrators, students, and staff to propose and pursue projects related to tolerance on campus. This fund was designed to offer partial or total funding for new projects, programs, and events that sought to establish common ground among various members of the university community. The design of the President's Common Ground Fund encouraged ideas, projects, and participation in a grassroots approach.

The project at Duke successfully contributed to the development and improvement of campus diversity initiatives and succeeded in implementing a broad range of them. The umbrella committee structure that was developed through the grant improved communication among the various university administrative offices doing diversity work. The project led to the establishment of comprehensive and collaborative efforts among the various administrative offices responsible for overseeing diversity initiatives. In addition, the funding process for student initiatives was streamlined, following the Common Ground Fund model. Discretionary accounts from Vice Provost for Academic Affairs and Dean of Trinity College, the Vice President for Student Affairs, and the President are now part of one funding system. "Diversity initiatives" is a new category for which students can request funds. The structure provided the needed flexibility to support creative initiatives across a broad university constituency.

B.   The Emerging National Mosaic

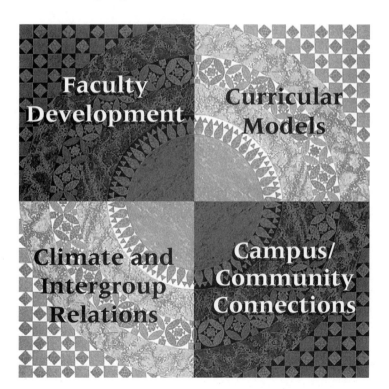

Four major areas have emerged in the 1980s and 1990s as central locales of diversity initiatives: faculty development, curricular models, climate and intergroup relations, and campus-community connections. These four pieces taken together assume a discernible pattern in the national mosaic of diversity work. When all six foundation- and corporation-supported diversity initiatives supporting this monograph are viewed as a collective portfolio of concerns, these same four areas with similar patterns emerge as dominant motifs.

1. Faculty Development

Because the heart of the academic enterprise is a knowledge base on which the intellectual activity of an institution rests, colleges, as part of their diversity effort, have chosen to invest heavily in faculty development as a way of examining the accuracy and range of that foundational knowledge. There is overwhelming consensus that it has been money well spent. Faculty who participated in such opportunities are, almost to a person, intellectually renewed, re-engaged in teaching, and delighted by a new-found collegiality with professional peers across many disciplines. Immersion in the extensive scholarship about diversity produced over the past three decades has raised critical disciplinary and interdisciplinary questions, reinvigorated traditional fields, defined ground-breaking new fields, and revised earlier understandings, assumptions, and previously unexamined "givens." Because faculty members typically teach what they already know, they need the opportunity to intensively study the developing scholarship of diversity. Most successful curriculum revisions have occurred after a critical core of faculty themselves have studied sufficiently to acquire a deeper expertise, and where professors have had sustained conversations with one another over time about the nature and purpose of curricular change.

Brandeis University and the University of Maryland sponsored five-week summer seminars for groups of fifteen faculty. Haverford College held weekly two-hour discussions during the semester. Hiram College paired individual faculty members with a scholar at another institution, who served as mentor. At Tulane University individual faculty members received stipends to support independent study. Bemidji University brought faculty from several institutions together for four one-day workshops, two of which were held at a local Indian reservation. Northern Michigan University also conducted workshops designed to emphasize the traditional values, ways, and beliefs of American Indians.

Most institutions offer stipends. In some cases they are equivalent to what a faculty member would earn teaching a summer course. More typically, it is far less. Some, such as Northern Michigan University and Mount Saint Mary's College, offer travel stipends, while others give book stipends with bibliographies and readings. Some opt to bring in visiting scholars, offer special lectures, or plan colloquia and forums. Whatever the model, it is vital that professors have multiple entry points for engaging with the new scholarship.

As the demand for training in the new scholarship of diversity increased, a number of free-standing institutes, workshops, and faculty development opportunities have been established by organizations that already had a reputation among their peers for offering highly respected curriculum and pedagogy training. The Washington Center for Improving the Quality of Undergraduate Education, for example, known for its pioneering work on teaching, has become a focal point for statewide workshops, conferences, and summer institutes that train faculty from institutions across the state. A similar state-focused organization is the New Jersey Project on Inclusive Scholarship, Curriculum, and Teaching, established in 1985, that offers workshops, conferences, institutes, and resources. A more regionally based organization, the Great Lakes College Association (GLCA), continues to provide a regular summer workshop on the multi-cultural curriculum, at which faculty revise an existing course and explore new pedagogical strategies. While most participants are from GLCA member colleges, some are from other institutions as well. Similarly, every June the Center for Research on Women at the University of Memphis conducts a four-day institute on curriculum transformation that is open to faculty nationwide.

In the national arena, the Association of American Colleges and Universities held a ten-day summer institute for nearly 200 faculty each year in 1994 and 1995, "Boundaries and Borderlands: The Search for Recognition and Community in America." AAC&U continues to convene regular conferences and institutes each year on diversity and learning. Furthermore, in a partnership with the University of Maryland, it has created DiversityWeb with on-line resources about the curriculum, institutional leadership, student development, and other topical issues (http://www.inform.umd.edu/diversityweb). DiversityWeb features *Diversity Digest*, a quarterly newsletter capturing the most innovative ideas from the field, and *Diversity Connections*, a directory of campus diversity projects.

A number of factors influence how successful faculty development initiatives are in reinvigorating faculty. Above all, faculty need to have the necessary time, focused study, and dialogue with their peers. Effective initiatives engage people in reading, thinking, and debating over time in a sustained group that fosters development of collegial and personal relationships. Learning about diversity is not a matter of merely adding a new book or module here and there. To the contrary, the scholarship is sophisticated, with insights typically challenging received understandings. Predictably, there is sometimes passionate disagreement about issues. As they debate ideas, faculty need a climate of openness, trust, and sustained dialogue with colleagues to work through to new understandings of sometimes competing truths.

Our site visits and reports to funding agencies reveal that as a group, faculty were effusive regarding faculty development reinvigorating their intellectual life. Many said that, in addition to changing their courses, their areas of research, and their relationships with colleagues, they were more confident teachers and took more risks with interactive and group projects. They also felt themselves more informed advisors to students. Ultimately, expanding a faculty member's knowledge base had an impact beyond a single course, frequently altering how a professor conceived of all courses. It also altered how faculty construed their role on the campus at large. Some, for example, who had participated in faculty development initiatives also described how they had become advocates for diversifying the faculty.

Faculty development initiatives proved most effective when they were part of a larger institutional commitment to and conversation about diversity. When the seminar, forum, or institute was endorsed and valued by the departments, programs, administrators, and the institution as a whole, the impact was likely to be more far-reaching and more lasting. Faculty were also less likely to feel tension about venturing into new fields that might not be valued later at promotion and tenure time.

2. Curricular Models

Curriculum development is, of course, inextricably tied to faculty development. The picture emerging nationally indicates that the new scholarship on diversity has influenced the shape and context of the academic curriculum. The evolving curriculum is far more diversified as it increasingly includes scholarship on diversity that has influenced almost every academic discipline. Much of that diversity scholarship represents new investigations of human history and culture previously regarded as insignificant or not regarded at all.

In some instances, diversity scholarship has been infused into already existing courses. Bethune Cookman College integrated diversity into their Freshman Orientation Course. In a management department, Northern Illinois University added a course, entitled Skill Development for Success in a Multicultural Environment, which examined stereotypes, belief systems, the nature of prejudice, and the importance of a multicultural work force.

In a recent analysis by the Association of American Colleges and Universities of the final self-evaluation reports from the ninety-two institutions in its curriculum and faculty development network, American Commitments: Diversity, Democracy, and Liberal Learning, more than half the schools in the project had implemented a diversity requirement. Most are broadly defined and include both world and U.S. diversity within one requirement. Others focus exclusively on domestic diversity using a comparative approach. Good examples can be found at the State University of New York at Buffalo in its general education requirement, "American Pluralism and the Search for Equality," a required course for all students, and at the University of California-Berkeley, in its American Ethnic Studies requirement. In each case, students must step outside the study of a single group and learn to compare groups in the context of the history of structured inequalities and prejudicial exclusion in the United States. At Buffalo, the course addresses race, class, gender, religion, and ethnicity; at Berkeley the focus is on race and ethnicity.

Another emerging curricular trend is the integration of community service into academic courses. Rutgers University and Hobart and William Smith Colleges both offer a sequence of courses on American pluralism and democratic citizenship that includes community service placements. The community service is not merely an add-on; these programs, often called "service learning," provide students intellectual preparation for the first-hand experience of working across cultural differences in a community setting. Students are encouraged to reflect on the experience systematically and to use the combination of experience and reflection to test and modify their initial frames of reference. Such curricular experimentation is deepening students' commitment to social responsibility. As they gain a deeper understanding of diversity and persistent inequalities, students more fully grasp the barriers that impede the development of strong communities on a local, national, and international level.

Long Island University implemented a service-learning model within the social sciences. The service-learning field experiences all take place within the Brooklyn community. Class assignments challenge the student to make intellectual connections between the theoretical and the practical realities of the service experience. As students explore diversity issues, they have an opportunity to examine their own and others' assumptions and biases.

Not surprisingly, curriculum revision has far more impact if it is part of a college-wide consensus. While curricular revisions reaching the greatest number of students are an integral part of general education programs, colleges and universities are increasingly realizing that having diversity introduced only in the freshman year or through a single course is insufficient. More institutions are, as a consequence, implementing curricular models that provide many different places and levels where students can revisit earlier understandings, explore new areas of inquiry, and connect knowledge about diversity to their majors.

Only about 10 percent of institutions in AAC&U's *American Commitments* initiative have opted for a required core curriculum in which all students take the same course. Such core courses usually demand that an institution come to a consensus about course content and learning goals. More typically, institutions choose the more flexible, if more diffuse, diversity requirement, in which many different courses from different departments can be designated as fulfilling the requirement. Politically such a model is also far easier to move through curriculum committees.

Another popular curricular model infuses diversity into existing curricula rather than creating a diversity course requirement. Unfortunately, some institutions underestimate how much faculty development such a curricular strategy requires. If, however, as at Bloomfield College, the commitment to infusion is accompanied by frequent opportunities for long-term faculty development, diversity then permeates the curriculum and students are more likely to engage critical issues about difference in nearly every course. The evaluation of the thirty schools in the Lilly project, *Improving Racial and Ethnic Diversity and Campus Climate at Four-Year Independent Midwest Colleges: An Evaluation Report of the Lilly Endowment Grant Program*, demonstrates that no single approach to the curriculum necessarily fits all institutions. Curriculum transformation can be done using any of the models discussed above.

Whatever the model, the emerging pattern for new diversity courses involves a comparative approach, integrating multiple differences within or across identity groupings, rather than the study of a single group (Humphreys 1997). More courses have begun to include systematic analysis of injustice, intolerance, inequality, and discrimination. More schools, especially those with religious missions like University of Detroit Mercy and Mount Saint Mary's College, are using diversity courses to explore moral and ethical questions. Students are challenged to use critical thinking skills in order to be able to take principled stands on controversial issues. To assist students' development in this area, courses have begun to include perspectives that acknowledge competing truths, so that students learn how to discern multiple perspectives even as they formulate their own position, a position informed by others but ultimately and distinctively their own.

Almost all faculty members who begin teaching diversity content soon become interested in the pedagogical issues that surface. Evidence suggests such courses lead to more student-centered learning, collaborative work, and interactive pedagogies. In one of the Lilly Endowment schools, for instance, the introduction of cooperative learning in a physics course placed students into multiracial work groups. The course not only stimulated more social contact among students interracially, but also increased the retention rate of students of color in science.

Several institutions have had extremely successful collaborations between students and faculty using research as the key link. California State University-Los Angeles, for example, organized five racially diverse faculty/student research teams. Their laboratory was the greater Los Angeles area, and the focus of the research was the city's extensive diversity. In an effort to stimulate interest in graduate study among students of color, Tulane University used some of its funds from the Ford Foundation to support summer research stipends for students whose work was guided by a Tulane faculty member. To Tulane's astonishment, fifty-two students applied for twelve slots. Faculty who participated as research advisors commented on how much they themselves learned through the process, not simply about new content in their fields but about the talents and ambitions of students of color on their campuses. In many cases, faculty described how they became new advocates for students of color in their departments.

3. Climate and Intergroup Relations

Introduced and made popular by Bernice Sandler in 1983 with her landmark, "The Chilly Climate for Women on Campus" (AAC 1983), "climate," referring to the overall environment on campus, has received much attention over the last three decades. As diverse student, staff, and faculty populations began to arrive on campuses, the climate was not always welcoming. Sometimes it was outright hostile. Soon educators began to see the correlation between campus climate and retention and between campus climate and educational success. Although each of the six funding agencies for campus diversity initiatives that were involved in this study included climate issues as part of their focus, three made it central: the Lilly Endowment, the William and Flora Hewlett Foundation, and the Philip Morris Companies Inc.

A range of activities was aimed at improving the climate. Typically those activities were directed to students, but several were concerned with faculty comfort levels, especially faculty of color. At Tulane University student groups submitted proposals for mini-programming grants and at Haverford College student leaders were trained in diversity issues so they could be change agents themselves. At the University of Iowa, the nationally ranked Forensic Union used external funds to develop topics and resources on race relations and cultural diversity; students raised provocative questions as they competed around the state, region, and nation. At Haverford College, workshops addressed the climate issues as experienced by the dining center staff, student athletic staff, deans and directors, student service staff, and public safety personnel. Columbia University held a town meeting entitled, "Black at Columbia: Building Common Ground," to open dialogue among students, faculty, staff, and alumni about being black in a predominantly white environment.

The emerging consensus is that before beginning any kind of diversity activities, it is important to conduct a formal assessment of the campus climate for diversity. Many available models can be adapted to specific institutions. (See the monograph in this series, *Assessing Campus Diversity Initiatives* and Smith, Wolf, and Levitan's *Studying Diversity in Higher Education*.) Such assessments, or audits, provide baseline data and show a snapshot of the terrain before decisions are made on any new programs. Audits allow an institution to identify pressing problems or particular groups who may be experiencing a hostile climate. Furthermore, a baseline allows an institution to measure progress over time and to identify the next most appropriate set of activities.

The most highly rated campus climate programs were careful to involve many elements of the campus; they were well-planned, with people directing them who had both the authority and the expertise necessary for the project. At Luther College, for instance, 29 percent of the total faculty and staff, that is, more than 150 people—faculty, maintenance workers, administrators, cafeteria workers, secretaries, resident life personnel—participated in a three-day workshop off campus in which they spent intensive time together receiving training on diversity issues. As a follow-up, the participants were assigned to clusters of six to eight people and challenged to initiate diversity activities as a small self-contained group. Three years later, some groups were still functioning, and members of those that had dissolved continued to identify their experience as a formative one in their lives. Reaching such a high percentage of people at the college created a tipping point, a momentum that eventually created a consensus about the value of diversity in the institution.

Another example of a very successful campus-wide experience occurred when a Midwestern college organized a set of diversity activities around the appearance on campus of an African American poet. Many people from almost every sector of the institution became involved in the planning before and after the poet's appearance. The college gave each employee a copy of one of the poet's books, enabling them to approach the poet's performance from a common starting point.

At the University of Redlands, through a Ford Foundation grant, a group of students organized a multicultural festival they called *Living on Common Ground*. It was so successful the first year, with students eager to assume leadership in it, that eventually the student government sponsored the festival. The event was further institutionalized when its funding was secured through a combination of student fees and university budget allocations. Each year the appeal and scope of the festival have increased. The local community, especially the local high school, has now become a partner in promoting and planning the festival. Planning it is a significant educational experience, and its content includes educational programs as well as the celebration of ethnic cultures.

Many have found that arts programs were especially successful, possibly because they create common entry points for participants. Even those were more successful, however, when they were well-planned and when a broad group of people had vetted the programs and felt invested in them. Poorly planned programs sometimes had negative consequences on climate even though intentions were admirable.

In the diversity projects aimed at changing campus climate, people have often discovered that it was more effective to target specific audiences for diversity programming rather than try to reach everyone with a more general program. There was, for example, greater success when a diversity training program was designed specifically for residence life staff or when an outside consultant worked only with faculty on teaching and advising.

4. Campus/Community Connection

Colleges have become increasingly aware of the communities around them as educational assets for their students and recognize the resources they themselves might invest in the communities. In the face of such a mutually beneficial situation, new partnerships are emerging between the campus and the community. These partnerships are sometimes initiated as an attempt to defuse town-gown tensions. In other cases, student interest in volunteer work has fueled relationships that help colleges turn outward.

One of the more successful projects to germinate from the confluence of several of these motivations occurred at Pitzer College, where grant funds were used to expand the small volunteer community service programs and hire a part-time coordinator. In the first year, ten students worked at eleven organizations in the community. By the end of the second year, the number of students had jumped to fifty and the organizations to thirty-three. The college then invested its own money to hire the coordinator full-time. The program has now expanded beyond offering volunteer experiences to integrating community service into academic courses. Another academic program has also evolved at Pitzer in which students have a "semester at home," living in a neighborhood not far from the college. The students serve as interns at a local multiracial elementary school where they assist teachers in conflict resolution.

Twenty institutions were funded through the Community Seminars in AAC&U's *American Commitments* initiative to form study/dialogue partnerships with community representatives. Despite modest grants of $3,000 each, matched by the institution, interest in applying for the grants was surprisingly high (three times as many institutions applied than there were grants), and the support internally within the campuses for these new ventures was remarkable. Among the most successful were those partnerships that had defined their projects together from the start, had some previous history of working together on other issues, and took the time needed to work through the differing viewpoints brought to the table.

An original and successful campus/community project was the Black History Archives Project at Virginia Commonwealth University (VCU). Its goal was to create an archival collection of historical research documents about the life of African Americans in the Richmond area. Before a single document was collected, however, the VCU administration, faculty, librarians and students invested a great deal of time visiting homes and creating trust and cooperation with various black community groups, a link that had not previously been cultivated by the university. As the project unfolded, black residents in Richmond came to see the archives as their own and began to donate a rich collection of documents. Because of its success locally, the project eventually expanded into the black community in Norfolk. The collection is also exposing students to expanded knowledge about America's racial history and culture.

In an unusual link between the campus and the community, some colleges invested in strengthening ties to the local community in order to diversify their student body. After two years, the investment paid off with increased recruitment and retention of students of color. One school also hired in the admissions office a new staff person who had deep ties to the community, resulting in applications from a new segment of the student population.

Finally, in an example of the community vicariously coming onto campus, Hiram College defused a potentially divisive situation when African-American students were supported through external funds to attend an off-campus speech by a controversial speaker. Instead of ignoring the tensions, Hiram students organized a forum led by the students who had heard the speaker. They discussed their response to the speaker and invited comments and questions from their student peers who had not attended. The climate invited openness, encouraged candid but constructive dialogue, and students were eager to learn across racial differences.

4

Pitfalls and Pinnacles: Campus Lessons

Because colleges and universities have been adopting diversity initiatives in innovative ways for more than two decades, many practitioners are clearer about where they have made mistakes and where they can measure successes. This chapter seeks to capture those campus insights. Culled from evaluations from many different institutions, the advice below represents the collective wisdom about what makes stronger, more effective single diversity projects as well as more comprehensive diversity initiatives. In the following section, "Advice from the Field," six areas are cited specifically: institutionalizing diversity; building consensus; engaging faculty; student development in the classroom; linking student and academic affairs; and networking. While each of these are individually significant, perhaps the most salient advice comes from those who over time understand the more powerful impact of creating synergy between the various individual efforts. The "Dimensions of Diversity" section of this chapter offers Daryl G. Smith's conceptual framework of the dimensions of diversity. By being attentive to the potential interface of these different dimensions, an institution can maximize the impact of their efforts and create more lasting change.

A.   Advice from the Field

1. Institutionalizing diversity initiatives

Building Diversity into Strategic Planning. As institutions grapple with re-structuring, downsizing, and doing more with less, many have turned to strategic planning. If, from the outset, diversity is a goal woven into strategic planning, diversity will then be a critical lens when discussing and planning any campus strategy whether recruitment, retention, or residence hall programming; whether hiring faculty, organizing athletic programs, or improving community relations. If an institution frames its mission as educating all of its students to live and thrive in a pluralist society, diversity is more likely to be integrated into the rest of the strategic planning. It is therefore a wise strategy to try to align diversity program goals with overall institutional goals.

In formulating an institutional diversity plan, clearly stated long-term and short-term goals emerging from campus dialogue across many locations are important. As the plan is being implemented, it is equally important to adjust or abandon any strategy that does not work.

Rich scholarship exists on theories of racial identity formation, feminist phase theories of intellectual development, and models of organizational development in diversity: these can be extremely useful when crafting diversity plans and charting progress.

Seeking the Greatest Institutional Impact. Colleges experienced in diversity planning find that initiatives have more impact when they are structured to incorporate multiple, simultaneous approaches that build momentum and eventually create a new campus ethos for diversity. Such an ethos is typically cultivated by conversation, consensus, knowledge, and common commitments. Many campuses have also benefited from conducting a campus diversity "audit" to provide a snapshot through which to identify both problem areas and success stories. Such unvarnished appraisals focus diversity initiatives and define pressing priorities.

New Staff Lines. Another mechanism that many institutions have turned to in order to institutionalize diversity is establishing new permanent positions. These often allow externally funded projects to continue after the life of a grant, or they create possibilities for initiating new programs. Spring Hill College in Alabama appointed a director of their newly established Multicultural Office, while in the admissions office, a California institution added a new line that brought on a person with long-standing connections to the community. It seems to be far more effective to make such new appointments full-time rather than part-time and to consider carefully to whom the staff person should report. If responsibilities include curriculum and faculty development, for instance, many have found it more effective to make the appointment in academic affairs rather than in student affairs. If responsibilities include student development and campus climate, more often the appointment is in student affairs. Several campuses stressed the importance of supporting the new appointment by continuing to assume that the daily responsibility for attending to diversity also belongs to the campus as a whole.

Advice From the Field

Institutionalizing Diversity Initiatives
  Build diversity into strategic planning
  Seek the greatest institutional impact
  Create new staff lines
  Create new faculty lines
  Include diversity in course descriptions
  Establish new academic programs
  Establish new structures with diversity as a central focus
  Add a diversity component to an already existing structure
  Create a diverse administrative team

Building Consensus and Considering Context
  Involve many people from a variety of campus locations to help plan, implement, evaluate, and sustain diversity initiatives
  Create opportunities for extensive debate and dialogue
  Solicit strong leadership from top administrators along with a strong base to accelerate momentum
  Share findings about diversity efforts to win public support and dispel misinformation

Engaging Faculty
  Appeal to the values of academic culture and faculty's role as a professional: the advancement of knowledge, the expansion of their intellectual expertise, and the improvement of teaching
  Provide multiple entry points for faculty to engage in intellectual and societal questions raised by diversity
  Seek creative, varied ways to generate dialogue in an atmosphere of genuine inquiry and mutual respect

Student Development in the Classroom
  Be attentive to how students respond to course material on diversity
  Provide students a series of structured, sequenced curricular opportunities to challenge them over time
  Permeate the curriculum both in general education and the major

Linking Student Affairs and Academic Affairs
  Develop stronger links to maximize resources, expertise, and impact
  Cultivate complementary and coordinated curricular and co-curricular programs
  Acknowledge the unequal status between the two while capitalizing on their differing expertise and purposes
  Provide a variety of forums and arenas, both curricular and co-curricular, where students can address these specific developmental issues

Networking
  Use networks to sustain diversity work, renew commitments, and expand knowledge
  Rely on multiple kinds of networks, both informal and formal, face to face or through technology
  Layer networks by linking with local, regional, national, and international

New faculty lines. Departments can institutionalize diversity by writing job descriptions that define expertise in diversity as part of the job requirement. They can also opt to create entirely new faculty lines, like the one at the University of South Florida in Third World women's studies or the University of Redlands' new faculty position in race and ethnicity. If faculty should leave from either kind of position, the expertise is retained in the job line; commitment to fill that slot is more likely to be consistently honored.

Course descriptions. Course descriptions in which diversity issues are explicit is another strategy for institutionalizing diversity in the curriculum. They reinforce the commitment to diversity as an educational priority for a department or the institution as a whole. Many campuses have incorporated diversity into general education requirements, the major, and electives.

New academic programs. One of the most common ways to guarantee that scholarly expertise in diversity will continue to be a permanent part of an institution's faculty profile has been to establish special studies programs where marginalized or underrepresented groups become visible. Women's studies programs, ethnic studies, and gay and lesbian studies programs, for example, often house diversity courses on a permanent basis and provide a continuing institutional vehicle for generating new courses. Such home departments also insure that a given school has a core of faculty with scholarly expertise in a given subject area and for whom research and teaching in diversity will continue to be a priority.

Northern Michigan University, for example, chose this option. While the state of Michigan has the tenth largest American Indian population in the United States, and Northern Michigan University has the largest number of American Indian students in a state university, there were few programs where students could deepen their knowledge of American Indians. With the commitment of a group of very dedicated faculty and administrators, the Center for Native American Studies was established as a regular budgeted program.

While some campuses wonder whether it might be better to transform the existing curriculum rather than to develop specialty areas, the presence of both can be educationally beneficial. Specialty areas provide expertise and a consistent source of scholarship. Complementing special studies, transformed courses in other disciplines ensure that key intellectual questions about diversity will be woven throughout the curriculum.

New structures with diversity as a central focus. In order to capitalize on the synergy among the variety of diversity activities, many campuses discovered that they needed an organizational structure to coordinate the wide-ranging work. A structure often marks the difference between disparate, low-impact, localized programming and collective, high-impact, pervasive programming. The University of Maryland, for example, found that a campus-wide Diversity Committee, advisory and accountable to the president, provides overall coherence to diversity work there. The English department at the University of Iowa created its own departmental diversity task force to examine issues of particular importance to their departmental goals. Rather than rely on an EEOC staff person outside the faculty, Brandeis University established a faculty diversity committee to assist departments in their search for diverse faculty members. Women's commissions like the one at the University of Michigan, composed of people from a wide variety of positions across the institution, have frequently proven to be effective structures for addressing the needs of women students, staff, faculty, and administrators. With new structures, however, clarifying goals, jurisdiction, and relation to pre-existing structures is needed to avoid confusion and internal competition.

Adding a diversity component to an already existing structure. An entirely new structure is not always necessary. To reconceive the goals and mission of an existing structure may be more logical and effective. For example, one campus added an admissions office staff person with special responsibility for recruiting more diverse students. Often already existing teaching and learning centers incorporate diversity as an important priority.

At Arizona State University West, for example, diversity in the classroom has become an integral part of a comprehensive faculty development program. Throughout the semester a series of videos address diversity in the classroom, business, and society. On the day after the screening, faculty members come together to discuss how to incorporate new ideas into their syllabi.

Davidson College added a minority counselor to its Counseling Center. The new counselor not only helps address the special concerns raised by the college's small population of students of color, but also plays an active role in education and outreach. The counselor meets with student groups, participates in orientation activities, and sponsors programs ranging from enhancing self-esteem to empowerment.

Creating a diverse administrative team. Multiple perspectives shared around the table generate better decision making and more informed policies. Denny's Corporation has had major problems dealing with diverse populations and, says President John A. Romandetti, "We recognized that our senior administrative team also had to be diverse in order to turn this company around." Many college and university presidents have likewise come to realize how important diversity is when building an administrative team. A diverse senior team signals to those making faculty and staff appointments that diversity is taken seriously. The goal of hiring a diverse faculty and staff turns spoken words into concrete actions taken by those in leadership positions.

2. Building Consensus and Communicating Results

Effective diversity initiatives engaged constituents from many different locations on campus to help plan, implement, evaluate, and do follow-up. Projects that relied exclusively on a tight, small core of planners who did not reach out to others had less impact.

Stronger projects were initiated after extensive debate and dialogue within the college, and many people were assigned responsibility for implementing plans. Strong leadership from top administrators working with a strong base of support accelerates the momentum and helps ensure the campus' full commitment.

Slow to realize the power of public communication, diversity practitioners have, for the most part, been put on the defensive by opponents of diversity. Since positive public attitudes toward their work are an invaluable support, it makes sense to cultivate public support through a systematic program of public communication. How both students and the country as a whole benefit from thoughtful attention to diversity in the higher education community and all of society is the good news that deserves to be spread. Disseminating findings and analyses not only wins public support for diversity work, but also dispels some of the misinformation about diversity and its outcomes.

3. Engaging Faculty

By appealing to the values of academic culture and their role as professionals, faculty are engaged most successfully. Faculty maintain curricular independence, and they are reluctant to participate in sensitivity training. Consequently, multiple entry points for faculty to engage intellectual and societal questions raised by diversity should be woven into any long-range planning. Not everyone will participate, but creating an intellectually compelling and participatory approach will appeal to the majority. Successful faculty initiatives avoided polarizing faculty opinions and sought creative and varied ways to generate dialogue in an atmosphere of genuine inquiry and mutual respect.

4. Student Development in the Classroom

Since diversity courses involve both the subject matter and response to that subject matter, to ignore pedagogical issues is to limit the effectiveness of courses. With diversity questions as with other intellectual issues, students need structured and sequenced curricular opportunities, consonant with a developmental model. As students become more sophisticated about diversity questions, the creation of timely challenges within courses and assignments, when strategically incorporated, can stretch them. Diversity in the curriculum is more effective when it permeates the curriculum both laterally (in several freshman courses) and vertically (in courses taken sequentially over several years.)

5. Linking Student Affairs and Academic Affairs

Links between student affairs and academic affairs need to be strengthened for resources and expertise to be maximized and for diversity efforts to have a pervasive impact on the campus. Since students live most of their lives outside the classroom, curricular projects can be greatly enhanced by connecting with co-curricular programming.

One program that has successfully bridged the divide between student affairs and academic affairs is the University of Michigan's Program on Intergroup Relations, Conflict, and Community (IGRCC). The IGRCC was conceived as a curricular-based initiative fully integrated with student affairs to link curricular and co-curricular programming with students' living/learning communities. For the past ten years IGRCC has worked closely with academic and student affairs units to develop undergraduate courses and mini-courses that include peer-facilitated discussions called Intergroup Dialogues. IGRCC also sponsors training practicums for student facilitators, First-year Interest Group Seminars (FIGS), student retreats, and Alternative Spring Breaks.

Students perceive and experience the world in dramatically different ways from faculty members or administrators. Whatever either of the latter groups does about diversity, most students are daily and personally living out the issues of diversity, in a sometimes confused way, often with pain, sometimes with eloquence and impressive resilience. It is therefore important for campuses to provide a variety of forums and arenas where students can address specific developmental issues. It matters, for example, that Jewish students have Hillel, that students of color have a multicultural center, or that women have a women's center. It matters as well that there also be areas for intergroup work across many differences, like ecumenical groups or interracial student alliances.

6. The Sustaining Value of Networking

Networks of every kind can help sustain diversity work, renew commitments, expand knowledge, and reduce the sense of loneliness. They can be as informal as potluck dinners or as formal as a national organization, as intimate as a group of colleagues known over time or as anonymous as a listserv. Some are internal to the workplace; others require leaving the workplace.

Long time diversity practitioners have strong networks, local and national, personal and professional. If there isn't a network locally, then create one. Regionally and nationally, there is a wider range of professional networks available. Many are organized as caucuses within traditional professional associations. Because of new technology, it is also possible to join an animated group of professional colleagues who care about diversity issues across a range of interests. For example, between listservs and Web sites, a person can be connected to colleagues who share the same concerns. Isolation can be replaced by connection with the flick of a finger on a computer key pad. AAC&U's DiversityWeb, created with assistance from the University of Maryland, is but one example of a national resource rich in material about campus practices and policies that also offers opportunities for exchange among diversity practitioners (http://www.diversityweb.org).

B. Dimensions of Diversity

If there is any single lesson emerging from the field, it is that individual diversity efforts have greater influence when they are part of an overall institutional design. Each locale, when seen in relation to one another and when drawing on the power of each other, becomes more than a lone, disconnected program. With the right synergy, diversity becomes pervasive rather than localized. In her research over the years, Daryl G. Smith has used the term "dimensions of campus diversity" as a way of discussing the importance of institutional interconnections in diversity efforts (Smith 1995). Her dimensions (pictured below) provide one way of visualizing that institutional mosaic.

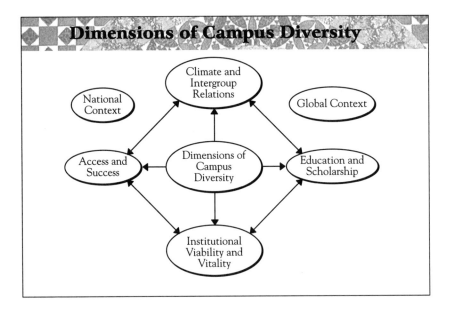

Smith includes four dimensions of diversity: access and success, campus climate and intergroup relations, education and scholarship, and institutional viability and vitality. The four represent locations on campus where attentiveness to diversity has occurred in this last half-century of significant experimentation with and commitment to diversifying higher education in the United States. They also highlight the main investigations of this monograph.

Access and success, expressed in phrases like recruitment, persistence, and retention, are principally concerned with inclusion of and achievement by previously underrepresented groups. Campus climate and intergroup relations focus on the kind of environment established and its influence on student success, faculty performance, and the well-being of staff who are employed there. Education and scholarship involve the inclusion of diverse traditions in the curriculum, the impact of diversity on teaching, and the effect of diversity on scholarly inquiry. Finally, the last dimension, institutional viability and vitality, asks the all-encompassing organizational question, "What would have to change if diversity were a central educational goal for our institution?"

While each of these four can organize tasks and be assessed discretely, their influence will be magnified if they work in relation to one another. Each will also be significantly weakened if its quadrant operates alone and not reinforced by the others. It is a matter of balance, of design, of arranging the individual pieces of the mosaic as part of a larger institutional blueprint. In discovering the appropriate balance among the four dimensions, an institution can more confidently craft its own distinctive vision.

Key to Progress: Reasons for Using Assessment in Diversity Work

In the twenty-first century, the nation and its educational institutions will have the most diverse population in its history. We have argued earlier that diversity in numbers alone does not guarantee that people understand, interact with, or can live productively with one another. Increasingly, people who previously could avoid contact, now work alongside each other in jobs, share social space in restaurants, malls, and movie theaters, and sit side-by-side in classrooms. Higher education has a major role in providing tools to transform proximity into relationship, to turn passive pluralism into engaged pluralism. Students on college campuses enter from all walks of life, full of hopes and aspirations. Already students of color, women, and returning adults comprise the majority of the population in higher education. Many of these students are first-generation students who see education as a pathway for educational, economic, political, and social mobility. The diversity efforts on campuses seek to ensure a clear path.

How do we know, however, which diversity efforts are effective and which need to be redesigned or scrapped? While some assessment research has been done, much more must be generated. What has been occasional must become commonplace. What has been spotty and individualized must become more comprehensive and seen in relation to one another.

Many who engage in diversity work believe that the work should speak for itself, because it is driven largely by the commitment to provide opportunity for all—the very premise upon which this country is founded. To measure intentions against accomplishment, campuses need to assess where they have been, where they are now, and where they want to go. Assessing diversity work means evaluating its worth, substantiating its benefits, correcting deficiencies, and validating its significance. Assessment can also document failures. Often failures mark the clearest pathway to a better way to do things. Assessment, therefore, provides a means of thinking through what, how, and why this work is being done.

At times, assessment underscores how mercurial diversity can be to assess. For example, a faculty member at Virginia Commonwealth explained that he had discovered that the discussion of race was difficult in the classroom because of the cultural context of the community. At first, he did not understand why students did not involve themselves in deep discussions. Eventually, he came to understand that for students from that part of the country, it was viewed as unseemly to discuss race in the presence of "mixed company." Learning and understanding this reality helped that professor design new strategies for helping students discuss race in such a context.

As crucial as assessment is to the improvement of the academy, the process itself often creates tensions and at times even fears. Assessment can create barriers. People are sometimes anxious about how to accurately measure learning or changes. Others worry that assessment will be used to undermine efforts, while still others fear that evaluation is not part of their expertise. The second monograph in our series, *Evaluating Diversity on College and University Campuses*, strives to mitigate these concerns by introducing readers to a variety of user-friendly approaches to evaluating diversity initiatives. By drawing on available research and proven instruments, the monograph illustrates how to assess diversity work, whatever one's subject matter or level of expertise in evaluation.

Why Invest in Assessment?

- Assessment helps an institution think strategically about its future.
- Data from assessments provide knowledge to inform educational work.
- Assessment can identify where unconscious bias that unnecessarily disadvantages particular populations might exist.
- Assessment deepens collegial work and creates community by bringing people into conversation to discuss, discover, and learn about their initiatives.
- Assessment helps maintain momentum and motivation.

But why must diversity initiatives be evaluated? Consider the following scenario. A president has just announced that the institution will be streamlining its commitments and mission. Like so many others, this institution is in the process of examining its goals, narrowing its scope, defining its niche, and eliminating everything that does not meet the new vision. How will a diversity initiative fare in such a context? Its fate is more protected if there is concrete, persuasive evidence indicating that diversity is critical to the institution's vitality. From another perspective, even without being driven by an external force, how can one know if a given diversity project is actually accomplishing its aims? A comprehensive assessment program offers the means by which to respond both to internal questions of accomplishment and external critics.

Assessment is a means for a college or university to think strategically about its future. How is diversity defined within the context of the institution? Whom does that institution serve? Who lives in the surrounding communities? How does the curriculum address the populations it serves? The responses to these and other questions should be part of any institution's strategic plan. Determining where the institution has been in relation to diversity work typically sets the stage for implementing appropriate new initiatives.

In *Students at the Center: Feminist Assessment*, for example, Suzanne Hyers discusses seven campuses that completed a three-year assessment of women's studies programs (Musil 1992). What is striking in her description is that each institution came to assessment from a different vantage point and with a different institutional history. Some, like the University of Missouri, soured by a rigid state-mandated evaluation that gave them little useful information, were seeking an assessment process that actually might answer some of their most pressing educational and programmatic questions. For others, like Hunter College, a more student-centered, faculty-driven assessment model allowed the assessment tools already in place to feed into a more holistic process that focused on curriculum, scholarship, and collective conversations. At Old Dominion University assessment provided an opportunity for the faculty to come to consensus on the goals of women's studies and to monitor how well they were achieving them. What emerged from the description of all seven institutions is that each institution's assessment was ultimately grounded in the institution's past, present, and future.

Evidence gathered about diversity initiatives can provide knowledge to inform further educational work. Assessment data can demonstrate whether programs are moving in the direction originally intended. These data also provide information for ongoing program improvement. For example, after an institutional audit was conducted, a university in the Midwest decided to conduct focus groups to determine if diversity issues were indeed becoming central to the college's mission. Because it was considered to be the most diverse state college in that state and had invested in a successful faculty development program, many believed that diversity issues had been resolved. The focus groups revealed that although the institution was indeed more diverse than ever, institutional norms and practices had not changed. Neither a diverse student body nor the diversity available through its geographic location altered the way the college orchestrated its business. In this case, assessment uncovered an unanticipated problem which permitted the institution to take steps to resolve it.

In response to this discovery, the institution created a presidential task force to develop policies and procedures that would serve the current student body. Student internships, for instance, had previously only been allocated to full-time students because faculty believed that part-time students with other commitments could not participate. Although the student population had changed from predominantly full-time to a part-time, adult population, no one had examined the implications of that shift for the institution's internship programs. More importantly, no one had asked the part-time students about their availability for internship programs within their field. In this case, the data not only informed but also charted new directions for institutional change.

Assessment research can also be helpful in identifying unconscious or deliberate bias that unnecessarily puts particular populations at a disadvantage. The SAT and ACT are prime examples that illustrate the limitations of what these examinations actually predict and the bias embedded in them. Although widely used as measurements of how selective institutions recruit their entering classes, research has demonstrated that the SAT and ACT, though useful, also have limitations, especially when test scores are set up as the single determinant (Wilds & Wilson 1998). While they accurately predict grades for majority men in the first year of college, women, for instance, tend to score lower than their male counterparts and yet get slightly higher freshman grades than their SAT or ACT scores would indicate. Good assessment helps practitioners eliminate barriers to student success.

Administrators may avoid assessing some aspects of diversity because they fear it will generate controversy. Diversity doesn't cause conflict; it uncovers it. Assessing diversity, then, simply reveals what lies beneath the surface. The assessment of gay and lesbian issues at one campus, for instance, demonstrated how ill-informed most students were; controversy was simply unmasked. In this case, assessment merely underscored the need to educate students about issues already fracturing relationships.

Assessment also brings people into conversation about what they are learning. In the process of such conversations, assessment can deepen collegial work and create community. Discussing the progress of programs brings people together to talk about how to assess work, improve initiatives, and identify issues that need to be modified, deleted, or restructured. It is common to be so involved in a program that one can sometimes lose sight of its ultimate goals. Conversations about assessing programs can help people collectively focus on the outcomes of their work.

Evaluation can also help maintain momentum. At Spring Hill College, for example, one staff member said, "The fact that an outside evaluator is here discussing our program and what we have achieved is a good thing. The visit provides time for us to get together and think about what we have accomplished. We live such hectic lives that we get pulled in many different directions and all we want to do is get the job done."

A campus need not wait to begin assessing its diversity work. The broader campus dialogue can begin immediately, a dialogue in which more focused investigations can eventually take place. As a starting point for campus conversations, the following set of questions can assist:

1. *What are the operating understandings of diversity? What are the emerging definitions? How is diversity understood in the context of its emerging definitions?*

2. *How is diversity understood in the context of the institution's immediate community? How does the institution's knowledge of diversity correlate with the actual demographics of its city and state, the country, and the world?*

3. *How is diversity understood in relation to the institution's particular historic and current context?*

4. *How has diversity been integrated into the institution's mission, vision, goals, and objectives?*

5. *What thought has been given to the ways students are taught to think about diversity, in curriculum, climate, or campus ethos?*

6. *How, over time, has the institution come to understand its current diversity climate?*

7. *What are some reasons that would persuade people on campus to document diversity initiatives? What tools would help them do it?*

Recommending campus dialogue about these seven questions is intended to foster a climate of expectation and openness to focused and sustained evaluation of diversity initiatives. There is an urgency about initiating such conversations and promoting more project and program specific evaluations in order to improve what is already underway. In a period of fiscal constraints, it is also expedient to identify new areas in which to invest institutional resources. Ironically, at the very historical moment when there is a shared rhetorical commitment to diversity in higher education, there has also been a very concerted attack on such efforts The assault flies in the face of evidence that the public, though it fears diversity might threaten national unity, also believes higher education can produce greater unity among differing cultures, people, and value commitments. The assault also contradicts the growing consensus that diversity helps the academy do its work even better. Nonetheless, the critique too often dominates the air waves and newsprint. It is time to tell the untold story of diversity's success on campus.

Contrary to many academicians' fears, then, assessment can support rather than undermine diversity work by both building stronger diversity initiatives and providing evidence to counter its critics. In light of California's Proposition 209 and similar legal setbacks to affirmative action, it is critical to communicate—to the court of public opinion as well as the court of law—the achievements of diversity. The assault on diversity work underscores the urgency of educating, communicating, and responding with data, evidence, illustrations, and stories.

Assessment, then, provides institutions with a means of documenting their own progress as well as accepting accountability. It can be a mechanism for achieving equal opportunity and keeping such a goal at the heart of the educational mission. The academy holds the promise of offering spaces of encounter and engagement, spaces that teach students how to deliberate in the face of difficult differences and how to expand their horizons by drawing on the deep resources diversity offers. In the process, students become more prepared to be informed citizens facile in working and living in a diverse democratic society like the United States. Assessing the value of diversity can therefore help higher education meet its fundamental intellectual and societal obligations. We hope this monograph and its two companion pieces help educators attend to that all-important task.

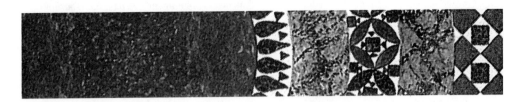

Bibliography

Astin, A.W. 1993. *What matters in college? Four critical years revisited.* San Francisco: Jossey-Bass Publishers.

Carter, D. J. and Wilson, R. 1997. *Minorities in higher education. Fifteenth annual status report 1996-97.* Washington, D.C.: American Council on Education.

Collins, P.H. 1991. *Black feminist thought: Knowledge, consciousness, and the politics of empowerment.* NY: Routledge, Chapman and Hall, Inc.

Desruisseaux, P. 1997. Foreign enrollment rises slightly at colleges in the United States. *The Chronicle of Higher Education,* December 12.

Dewey, J. 1927. *The public and its problems.* Athens, OH: Swallow Press.

Dey, E.L. and Hurtado, S. 1994. College students in changing contexts. In P. Altbach, R. Berdahl and P. Gumport, eds. *Higher education in American society.* Amherst, NY: Prometheus.

DYG, Inc. 1998. *The Ford Foundation Campus Diversity Initiative national poll gauging public attitudes towards diversity in higher education.* NY: DYG, Inc.

Elway Research, Inc. 1998. *The Ford Foundation Campus Diversity Initiative survey of Washington businesses.* Seattle, WA.

Herbst, J. 1982. *From crisis to crisis: American college government 1636-1819.* Cambridge, MA: Harvard University Press.

Hilliard-Jones, A. 1996. Diversity: A global business issue. *Fortune.* April 15.

Hodgkinson, H.L. 1992. *A demographic look at tomorrow.* Washington, D.C.: Center for Demographic Policy. Institute for Educational Leadership.

hooks, bell. 1984. *Feminist theory: From margin to center.* Boston, MA: South End Press.

Horowitz, H.L. 1987. *Campus life: Undergraduate cultures from the end of the eighteenth century to the present.* Chicago: University of Chicago Press.

Humphreys, D. 1997. *General education and American commitments: A national report on diversity courses and requirements.* Washington, D.C.: Association of American Colleges and Universities.

Humphreys, D., ed. 1998. *Diversity Digest,* Washington, D.C.: Association of American Colleges and Universities, vol. 1.

Hune, S. 1998. *Asian Pacific American women in higher education: Claiming visibility and voice.* Washington, D.C.: Association of American Colleges and Universities.

Hyers, S. 1992. Voices from the campuses. In Caryn McTighe Musil, ed. *Students at the center: Feminist assessment.* Washington, D.C.: Association of American Colleges and Universities.

Justiz, M.J., Wilson, R., Bjork, L.G. 1994. *Minorities in higher education.* Washington, D.C.: American Council on Education/ORYX Press.

Levine, L.W. 1996. *The opening of the American mind: Canons, culture, and history.* Boston, MA: Beacon Press.

Musil, C.M., ed. 1992. *The courage to question: Women's studies and student learning.* Washington, D.C.: Association of American Colleges and Universities.

Nettles, M.T. and Perna, L. 1997. *The African American education data book. Volume I: Higher and adult education.* Virginia: The College Fund/United Negro College Fund.

Port, S.T. and Yachnin, J. 1998. A more perfect union. *The Michigan Daily,* February 13.

Pratt, M.L. 1990. *Arts of the contact zone.* Unpublished keynote address at the Modern Language Association Literary Conference, Pittsburgh, Pennsylvania.

Sandler, B. 1983. *The chilly climate for women on campus.* Washington, D.C.: Association of American Colleges and Universities.

Sedlacek, W.E. 1995. *Improving racial and ethnic diversity and campus climate at four-year independent Midwest colleges: An evaluation report of the Lilly Endowment Grant Program.* College Park: University of Maryland, p.109.

Solomon, Barbara Miller. 1985. *In the company of educated women: A history of women and higher education in America.* New Haven, CT: Yale University Press.

Smith, D.G. 1995. Organizational implications of diversity in higher education. In M.M. Chemers, S. Oskamp and M.A. Costanzo, *Diversity in organizations: New perspectives for a changing workplace.* Thousand Oaks, CA: Sage Publications.

Smith, D.G., Wolf, L.E., and Levitan, T. 1994. *Studying diversity in higher education. New directions for institutional research,* 81. San Francisco: Jossey-Bass Publishers.

The Ford Foundation Campus Diversity Initiative. 1998. *Washington state public opinion poll on diversity in higher education coverage report.* Washington, D.C.: PR Solutions, Inc.

The Mortenson Research Seminar on Public Policy Analysis of Opportunity for Postsecondary Education. 1997. Family income by educational attainment, *Postsecondary education opportunity*, Oskaloosa, IA:, no. 64, October.

U.S. Bureau of the Census, Current Population Reports Series. 1998. *Population profile of the United States: 1997*. Washington, D.C.: U.S. Government Printing Office, p.23-194.

U.S. Department of Education, National Center for Education Statistics. 1995. *The condition of education, 1995*. Washington, D.C.: U.S. Government Printing Office.

U.S. Department of Education, National Center for Education Statistics. 1997. *Digest of education statistics, 1997*, NCES 98-015, by Thomas D. Snyder. Production Manager, Charlene M. Hoffman. Program Analyst, Claire M. Geddes. Washington, D.C.: U.S. Government Printing Office.

Wilds, D.J. and R. Wilson. 1998. *Minorities in higher education 1997-98*. Washington, D.C.: American Council on Higher Education.

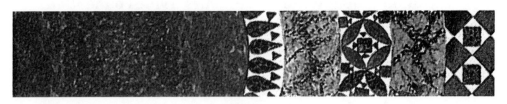

Appendix

Colleges and Universities That Received Grants
from the Five Foundations and One Corporate
Philanthropic Program for the Specific Diversity
Initiatives Named in this Monograph

Institutions Supported By The James Irvine Foundation
Diversity Grant Program
1987–1997
[20]

Art Center College of Design

California College of Arts and Crafts

California Institute of the Arts

California Institute of Technology

California Lutheran University

The Claremont Graduate University

Dominican College of San Rafael

Harvey Mudd College

Holy Names College

Loyola Marymount University

Mount Saint Mary's College

Occidental College

Pepperdine University

Saint Mary's College Santa Clara University

Stanford University

University of La Verne

The University of San Diego

The University of San Francisco

University of Southern California

Western Association of Schools and Colleges

Institutions Supported By The Ford Foundation Grant Program, "The Campus Diversity Initiative" 1990–1999
[294]

Albany College of Pharmacy-Union University

Albany Law School

Albany Medical College of Union University

Albany State University

Albion College

Antioch College

Antioch University

Antioch University - Seattle

Arizona State University

Arizona State University West

Arrowhead Community Colleges

Augsburg College

Augustana College

Avila College

Bacone College

Baldwin-Wallace College

Bard College

Barry University

Bates College

Baylor University

Bellevue Community College

Beloit College

Bemidji State University

Benedictine University

Bentley College

Bethune-Cookman College

Big Bend Community College

Bismarck State College

Blackfeet Community College

Bloomfield College

Boise State University

Boston College

Bowie State University

Bowling Green State University

Brandeis University

Brookdale Community College

Brown University

California State Polytechnic University

California State University Los Angeles

California State University Long Beach

Carleton College

Carlow College

Central Washington University

Centralia College

Chapman University

Chemeketa Community College

Clackmanas College

Coe College

Coker College

Colby-Sawyer College

College Misericordia

College of Charleston

College of New Jersey

College of Saint Rose

College of Southern Idaho

Colorado College

Columbia College

Columbia College - Chicago

Community College of Denver

Community College of Philadelphia

Community Colleges of Baltimore County Essex

Cornell College

County College of Morris

CUNY Brooklyn College
CUNY City College
CUNY Hunter College
CUNY Queens College
Denison University
DePauw University
Dickinson State University
Dillard University
Duke University
Earlham College
Eastern Idaho Technical College
Eastern Nazarene College
Eastern New Mexico University
Eastern New Mexico University-Roswell
Edmonds Community College
Emory University
Fairfield University
Fairleigh Dickinson University
Fergus Falls Community College
Ferris State University
Florida International University
Florida Memorial College
Fort Hays State University
Georgetown University
Green River Community College
Grinnell College
Hampton University
Hartwick College
Harvard University
Haverford College
Heritage College
Hiram College
Hobart and William Smith Colleges
Hope College
Hudson Valley Community College
Huston-Tillotson College
Idaho State University
Illinois Benedictine
Illinois Wesleyan University

Indiana State University
Indiana University Purdue University Fort
     Wayne
Indiana University Kokomo
Indiana University Northwest
Indiana University South Bend
Iowa State University
Itasca Community College
Johnson C. Smith University
Kalamazoo College
Kean University
Keene State College
Kellogg Community College
Kenyon College
Knox College
Lake Forest College
Lane Community College
Lawrence Tech University
Lawrence University
LeMoyne-Owen College
Lewis and Clark College
Lincoln University
Livingstone College
Lock Haven University
Los Angeles Southwest College
Lower Columbia College
Luther College
Macalester College
Maria College of Albany
Marymount College
Marymount Manhattan
Marywood University
Massachusetts College of Liberal Arts
Miami-Dade Community College
Michigan State University
Middlesex Community College
Millikin University
Millsaps College
Minneapolis Community College

Mississippi State University

Monmouth College

Montgomery College Rockville Campus

Morehead State University

Morgan State University

Morris College

Mount Hood Community College

Mount Saint Mary's College, LA

Mount Union College

National Hispanic University

Nebraska Wesleyan University

New School for Social Research

New York University

Norfolk State University

North Carolina A&I State University

North Carolina State University

North Dakota State University

North Idaho College

North Seattle Community College

Northeastern Illinois University

Nova Southeastern University

Oakwood College

Oberlin College

Occidental College

Ohio State University

Ohio Wesleyan University

Olivet College

Olympic College

Onondaga Community College

Pace University

Pacific University

Palm Beach Atlantic College

Pasadena City College

Pitzer College

Princeton University

Ramapo College of New Jersey

Randolph-Macon Woman's College

Rensselaer Polytechnic Institute

Ripon College

Rocky Mountain College

Rogue Community College

Rowan University

Rust College

Rutgers University-State University of
    New Jersey

Saint Edward's University

Saint Francis College

Saint Lawrence University

Saint Leo College

Saint Louis Community College at Forest
    Park

Saint Michael's College

Saint Olaf College

Saint Thomas University

San Francisco State University

San Juan College

Santa Ana College

Schenectady County Community College

Seattle Central Community College

Seattle University

Shoreline Community College

Siena College

Simmons College

Skagit Valley College

Skidmore College

South Puget Sound Community College

Southern Illinois University Edwardsville

Southwest Texas State University

Spelman College

Spokane Falls Community College

Spring Hill College

Stanford University

Stillman College

SUNY A&T College at Cobleskill

SUNY at Buffalo

SUNY College at Buffalo

SUNY College at Cobleskill

SUNY College at Cortland

SUNY College at Potsdam

SUNY Empire State College

SUNY Regents College

SUNY Stony Brook

SUNY University at Albany

Susquehanna University

Tacoma Community College

Temple University

Tennessee State University

Texas College

The College of Wooster

The Evergreen State College

The Sage Colleges

Tougaloo College

Trinity College

Tulane University

Tuskegee University

Union College

University of Arizona

University of California Berkeley

University of California Irvine

University of California Los Angeles

University of California San Diego

University of Central Florida

University of Chicago

University of Detroit-Mercy

University of Hawaii at Manoa

University of Houston

University of Idaho

University of Iowa

University of Maine

University of Maryland College Park

University of Massachusetts Boston

University of Massachusetts Lowell

University of Memphis

University of Miami

University of Michigan

University of Missouri Rolla

University of New Mexico

University of North Carolina Chapel Hill

University of North Carolina Greensboro

University of North Dakota

University of Northern Iowa

University of Notre Dame

University of Pennsylvania

University of Redlands

University of Scranton

University of Texas Arlington

University of Virginia

University of Washington - Bothell

University of Washington - Seattle

University of Washington - Takoma

University of Wisconsin Colleges

University of Wisconsin Madison

University of Wisconsin Stevens Point

Valparaiso University

Vassar College

Vermilion Community College

Virginia Commonwealth University

Wabash College

Wagner College

Washington State University

Wayne State University

Wesleyan University

Westchester Community College

Western Washington University

Whitworth College

Wilkes University

William Paterson University of New
Jersey

William Rainey Harper College

Worthington Community College

Xavier University

Yakima Valley Community College

Yale University

Youngstown State University

Institutions Supported By The Lilly Endowment Grant Program, "Improving Racial And Ethnic Diversity And Campus Climate At Four-Year Independent Midwest Colleges"
1991–1994
[40]

Antioch University

Aquinas College

Barat College

Bradley University

Cardinal Stritch College

Cleveland Institute of Art

College of Mount Saint Joseph

College of Saint Francis

Columbia College

DePauw University

Fontbonne College

Grinnell College

Hiram College

Indiana Institute of Technology

Iowa Wesleyan College

Kenyon College

Lawrence University

Lewis University

Luther College

MacMurray College

Marquette University

Madonna University

Midway College

Millikin University

North Park College

Northland College

Notre Dame College

Ohio Dominican College

Ohio Wesleyan University

Park College

Saint Ambrose University

St. Louis University

Saint Mary's College

Saint Norbert College

Saint Xavier University

Siena Heights College

Stephens College

Valparaiso University

Wabash College

Xavier University

Institutions Supported By The Philip Morris Companies, Inc. Program "Tolerance On Campus: Establishing Higher Ground" 1992–1995

[11]

Bethune-Cookman College
Colby College
Columbia College-Columbia University
Davidson College
Duke University
Haverford College
Long Island University
Northern Illinois University
Northern Michigan University
Occidental College
University of Wisconsin-Oshkosh

Institutions Supported By The William And Flora Hewlett Foundation Grant Program, "Pluralism And Unity" 1994–1999

[52]

Bard College

Bates College

Bowdoin College

Bryn Mawr College

California State University at Northridge

Clark University

Colgate University

Columbia University

Dartmouth College

Depauw University

Dickinson College

Franklin Pierce College

Gallaudet University

Graduate Theological Union

Haverford College

Heritage College

Heritage College

Hobart and William Smith Colleges

Johns Hopkins University

Knox College

Loyola Marymount University

Mount Chalon Saint Mary's College

Muhlenberg College

Oberlin College

Occidental College

Pomona College

Smith College

Stanford University

Swarthmore College

The University of California at Berkeley

The University of California at Davis

The University of California at Irvine

The University of California at Los
Angeles

The University of California at Riverside

The University of California at San Diego

The University of California at San
Francisco

The University of California at Santa
Barbara

The University of California, Santa Cruz
Foundation

The University of Massachusetts at
Amherst

The University of Michigan

The University of North Carolina at
Chapel Hill

The University of Redlands

The University of Rhode Island

The University of Southern California

The University of Texas at Austin

The University of Washington

The University of Washington

Wake Forest University

Washington State University

Wellesley College, Wellesley

Wesleyan University

Whitman College

Institutions Supported By The W.K. Kellogg Foundation Grant Program, "Centers Of Excellence" 1994–1997 [10]

Clark Atlanta University

Fisk University

Florida Agricultural and Mechanical University

Hampton University

Howard University

Morehouse College

North Carolina Agricultural and Technical State University

Spelman College

Tuskegee University

Xavier University